JESUS AS COUNSELOR

JESUS AS COUNSELOR

ROBERT C. LESLIE

ABINGDON • Nashville

Jesus as Counselor

A Festival Book

Copyright © 1965 by Abingdon

All rights reserved

Festival edition published May 1982

ISBN 0-687-19930-1

Previously published as *Jesus and Logotherapy* under

ISBN 0-687-19927-1

PRINTED IN THE UNITED STATES OF AMERICA

To my father,
who lives the Scriptures

PREFACE

The case study approach has been used extensively in the social sciences, but has seldom been applied to biblical material. The personal ministry of Jesus, however, lends itself very well to the case study approach, especially when the major interest is not so much in specific details as it is in timeless truths. Since the underlying principles of personal relationships are often lost sight of in the familiar Gospel narrative, a psychological system in the contemporary psychotherapeutic world has been employed to throw new light on selected incidents. The particular system chosen is the logotherapy of Viktor E. Frankl.

The ministry of Jesus was always concerned more with life transformation than with therapy. The basic purpose of Jesus was always centered in relating a person more directly with God. However, when his approach is studied in the light of current psychological principles, it becomes apparent that the methodology he used illustrates many of the principles uncovered by contemporary psychotherapy, especially when the therapy follows the general line of an approach like Frankl's.

The focus in these studies will center, as good biblical study always does, on the basic principles underlying the specific accounts rather than on the minute details of the event. That is, we will be less interested in the details of the incident in its first century setting than in the relationships between people which are timeless and hence directly relevant. Although critical New Testament scholarship has been taken into account, our purpose here is less critical than it is therapeutic; that is, we are concerned with finding in the various incidents hints about personal relationships that are directly and immediately applicable to daily living.

The biblical incidents selected are accepted pretty much at face value, even though modern scholarship makes it clear that the records have suffered in transmission and that authenticity is sometimes questionable. For our purpose, however, the survival of these reports after so many centuries speaks to their authenticity as descriptions of types of human experience shared in common by many. As such, they become useful material for exploration, even though details are missing and condensation and modification have obviously taken place. The one question regarding authenticity which is deemed particularly relevant might be phrased as follows: Is this account consistent with the method and spirit of Jesus as revealed in the major trends of the New Testament account?

Any study of interpersonal relationships necessarily implies both a technique of counseling and a doctrine of man. This study will draw heavily on the approach in psychotherapy evolved by psychiatrist Viktor E. Frankl, M.D., in Vienna,

under the name "logotherapy," the "therapy of meaning."
Tested in the rigors of concentration camp living, logotherapy
offers a philosophy of life and a method of counseling which is
more consistent with a basically Christian view of life than any
other existing system in the current therapeutic world. Frankl is
a Jew, but his point of view is broader than any sectarian
approach.

Viktor Frankl, who was born in 1905, holds the degrees of
Doctor of Medicine and Doctor of Philosophy from the
University of Vienna, where he is Professor of Psychiatry and
Neurology. He is also the head of the Department of Neurology
at the Poliklinik Hospital in Vienna. He has lectured on most of
the major university campuses in the United States. It was my
privilege to study with him in Vienna for nine months in
1960-61.

Although the main purpose of this book is to come to a better
understanding of how Jesus characteristically worked with
people, the work of Frankl has been introduced in a logical order
which sets forth the outline of his therapeutic approach. Thus
while each chapter stands as a unit in itself and demonstrates a
specific feature of the ministry of Jesus, the unfolding of Frankl's
logotherapy provides a unifying strand. The chapter headings
are drawn largely from Frankl's terminology.

It will become clear that Frankl builds his system on the
foundation provided by depth psychology (particularly psychoanalysis), but his modifications are so basic that a whole new
orientation is given to the understanding of man. In my work as a
teacher of adult classes, as a professor in a theological school,
and as a counselor in problems of marriage and personal adjust-

ment, I have found Frankl's orientation especially helpful. In relating the truths of Christianity to everyday living, Frankl's system provides a useful handle.

ROBERT C. LESLIE

March, 1968
Pacific School of Religion
Berkeley, California

CONTENTS

I. Exploring Height Psychology 13

  The Temptations of Jesus; Luke 4:1-13

II. Mobilizing the Defiant Power
  of the Human Spirit 24

  Zacchaeus; Luke 19:1-10

III. Finding the Personal Life Task 36

  The Rich Young Ruler; Mark 10:17-22

IV. Filling the Existential Vacuum 47

  The Samaritan Woman; John 4:4-27

V. Resolving Value Conflicts 55

  The Paralyzed Youth; Mark 2:2-12

VI.   Actualizing the Self
      in Responsible Commitment 64
      Simon the Pharisee; Luke 7:36-50

VII. Realizing Creative Values 74
      *Peter; Matthew 16:13-19; Luke 22:31-34,
      54-62*

VIII. Realizing Experiential Values 84
      Mary and Martha; Luke 10:38-42

IX.   Realizing Attitudinal Values 92
      The Bethesda Invalid; John 5:2-15

X.   Restoring Man's Dignity 102
      The Gerasene Demoniac; Mark 5:1-20

XI.   Exercising Man's Freedom 112
      Jesus as Servant; John 13:3-5, 12-16

      Notes 125

      Index 135

I. Exploring Height Psychology
The Temptations of Jesus; Luke 4:1-13

A classic description of the internal struggle going on in each man's soul is given in the record of the temptations of Jesus. The temptation experience is not only a clarification of the principles by which Jesus chose to govern his own life; it is also an account of the basic choices that confront every man as he steps from the shelter of the family into the arena of life. By establishing some fundamental guidelines in the major areas of choice, everyday decisions become subject to principles rather than to personal whim. Having established in advance the basic principles by which life will be lived, the individual is freed from the necessity of agonizing over each decision, or of leaving his course of action to pure chance. Indeed, a distinguishing feature of maturity is the refusal to act purely on the basis of expediency; each act is decided upon by reference to principle.

A basic insistence of the Christian faith is that man is free to make his decisions consciously. Without discounting the influence of unconscious factors operating in a person's life, Christianity nevertheless asserts, in an unqualified way, that the ultimate outcome of man's adventure in life depends upon his personal response. Whatever unfortunate experiences have come to him in life, the decisive factor lies not in the conditions but in the personal response to them. Psychiatrist Viktor E. Frankl describes the religious man as the one who says "yes" to life; as the man who, in spite of anything that life brings, still faces his existence with a basic conviction in the worthwhileness of life.[1]

To be sure, one of the major contributions of depth psychology has been to point out how powerful unconscious forces are and how early our life orientation tends to be formed. It is well known that Sigmund Freud attached major signficance to the preschool years and was convinced that the patterns for life were established before the broadening school experience was entered upon. Even though we cannot accept this deterministic viewpoint of Freud without serious modification, we must nevertheless recognize that, unconsciously, the child absorbs ("introjects") the standards of the most significant persons who surround him in early life, and that in the normal course of events his feeling about himself and his world is pretty well formed by the time he enters junior high school. Without the child's realizing it, the emotional foundation for later conscious decisions has been laid.

It is the task of later adolescence and of early adulthood, however, to make conscious the orientation by which adult life will be directed. A major aspect of the adolescent's striving for selfhood ("ego-identity," to use the descriptive term of Erik Erikson) revolves around the value system which he appropriates, the conscious decisions which he makes. Indeed, a major value in "bull sessions" or discussions of any sort is that opportunity is provided to think out loud about the major direction that one needs to take for his life. That the older adolescent (late teens) needs to be exposed to the claims of religion on his life at this time is quite obvious, for if his loyalty is not captured by a God-centered view of life it will be ensnared in secular values.

To be sure, the God-centered view of life has been severely challenged by the reductionism of a scientific view which reduces everything to its earliest origins and its most primitive forms. But the very task of religion is to look beneath the level of facts to the deeper dimensions of life. One of the chief values of studying the biblical record is that here, in symbolic ways, the deepest experiences of man, including his efforts at opening the channels between himself and the suprahuman world, are presented in graphic form. The persistent biblical image of man responding to God's call is the dramatic way of saying that conscience is more than an introjected parental admonition; it is also man reaching out to realize the full potential for which he was created. As Frankl puts it, "Conscience is the voice of transcendence; man intercepts the voice but does not originate it." [2]

Man's struggle to realize his potential, and the demoniac forces that tempt him to settle for a lesser life, are vividly set forth in the record of the temptation of Jesus as recorded in Luke's Gospel (4:1-13). How could the demoniac temptations that face each person be more graphically presented than through the imagery of a dialogue with the devil! When these three temptations are recognized as basic questions with which every person is confronted, and to which answers have to be given, then the scriptural account becomes far more than only a presentation of the preparation of Jesus for his wider ministry. It is the story of Man who identifies the forces struggling within himself for mastery, who makes a conscious renunciation of these common temptations, and so lays down an orientation for his life that is based on a value system which will give meaning to all he undertakes.

However one attempts to define maturity, some kind of integrating principle must always be included. The temptations of Jesus illustrate vividly that the principle which made a unity out of the many facets of his personality was his reference of all matters of life to the dimension that included God. If one seeks to understand the source of his power, it was in his closeness to God. If one seeks to understand the patience of his ministry, it was in his constant seeking out of God. If one seeks to understand the courage of his single-heartedness, it was in his consciousness of the presence in his life of the spirit of God. But even more than this, the temptation experiences make clear to us the path by which he reached the unshakable sense of direction that characterized his whole ministry.

The first temptation which came to Jesus, and which is common to all of us, was to let the pleasure principle prevail, to satisfy immediate sensual desires without regard for any long-term goals. One needs only to recall how extreme hunger tends to blot out all other interests, or how severe pain tends to cancel out all other concerns, or how unseasonable extremes of temperature tend to reduce human efficiency to recognize how common this temptation is. To satisfy the urgent call of the body for freedom from hunger (physical or sexual), or pain, or cold is the common inclination.

Yet, evidence from many sources makes it crystal clear that the law of self-preservation is not the only law at work among men. Where there is a commitment to a life task, where there is an allegiance to a supreme value, *there* the point of view that insists that all higher values are dependent upon the satisfaction first of the most primitive drives is proved false.

The record of experiences in concentration and internment camps in World War II underscores this fact. Viktor Frankl, who survived two and a half years in four different concentration camps, insists that the evidence is quite clear: man *can* "escape the destiny of his social surroundings" even in the concentration camp setting. "Even in this socially limiting environment, in spite of this societal restriction upon his personal freedom, the ultimate freedom still remains his: the freedom even in the camp to give some shape to his existence." [3] Taking vigorous exception to environmental determinism, Frankl asserts:

It is in no way predetermined what the camp would make of one, whether one would become a typical "KZLer" [*Konzentrationslager-häftling*—concentration camp inmate] or whether one would, even in the state of duress, even in this extreme borderline situation of man, remain a human being. In each case this was open to decision. There can, therefore, be no question of a man's necessarily and automatically having to succumb to the impressing stamp of the camp atmosphere upon his character.[4]

When Frankl asserts that in the camps there were "plenty of examples—often heroic ones—to prove that even in the camps men . . . did not have to submit to the apparently almighty concentration camp laws of psychic deformation," [5] he is underscoring what Dorothy Thompson wrote after visiting Dachau

17

and studying the records of life there: "They who remained men, in conditions of lowest bestiality, served an Image and an Ideal higher than the highest achievements of man." [6]

Frankl describes how loss of hold on spiritual values allowed the animal-like characteristics to take over:

That which was ultimately responsible for the state of the prisoner's inner self was not so much the enumerated psychophysical causes as it was the result of a free decision. Psychological observations of the prisoners have shown that only the men who allowed their inner hold on their moral and spiritual selves to subside eventually fell victim to the camp's degenerating influences. [7]

Whereas the Freudian hypothesis of the all-pervasiveness of the pleasure principle has obvious evidence to support it in some cases, it turns out to be only an hypothesis and one based on selective evidence. Man simply does not live by bread alone; nor must his need for bread be satisfied before he can turn to meeting others' needs. Indeed the precept: "First survive, then philosophize about it," was invalidated in the camps. Frankl is very clear in stating that "what was valid in the camp was rather the exact opposite; . . . first philosophize, then die." [8] When man's way of life is one which invariably brings God into the picture, then the long pull becomes more important than the immediate desire.

The first temptation is so obviously present in all our lives that we need not linger with it. Who has not felt the pull of immediate personal pleasures, the fulfillment of which stands in the way of the larger, more obscure goal? Like Scarlett O'Hara in Margaret Mitchell's *Gone with the Wind*, it is easier to "think of that tomorrow" and so avoid facing the consequences of life lived for the pleasure of today. But the sobering words of Jesus make the matter very clear; when man's life is related to the word that God would say to him, then a new dimension is entered. When man's will is scrutinized alongside of God's will for him, then the picture is changed. And even though the search for God's will is never an easy one, the very fact of embarking on the search brings a new dimension of depth into daily life.

Thus to forego immediate gratification in the interest of future more worthwhile goals was the first decision that Jesus made. He would determine his line of action, not according to what seemed to hold out the most for him personally at the moment, but to what long-term goals required, as seen in the light of God's will for him. That it was not always easy for him to see what God's will was is made clear in the agonizing prayer in the Garden of Gethsemane, ending with the words, "Nevertheless not my will, but thine, be done" (Luke 22:42).

The second temptation which Jesus faced and which all of us face is to let the power principle prevail, to put personal ambition for status and prestige above all else. So far-reaching is this tendency that Alfred Adler saw in it the basic motivation in life. Several of the cultural analysts (Sullivan, Horney, Fromm), in stressing the importance of self-esteem, demonstrate how often personal status is sought through the power drive. None of us is wholly free from the temptation to exploit others in order to enhance his own position.

There is no denying the need for adequate self-esteem. It is quite clear, as psychoanalysis has helped us to understand, that before one can love his neighbor he needs to love himself "properly." [9] A positive relationship with a neighbor stems from a positive feeling about one's self. Rather than condemning a person for an unloving attitude toward others, we are beginning to realize that his real need lies in discovering greater worth in himself. It is a sad commentary on our impersonal society that many a self-depreciating person finds genuine acceptance only in a formal relationship with a therapist, and out of this relationship gains a more positive appraisal of himself.

Thus we have been helped by dynamic psychology to understand the difficulty that many have in being outgoing, loving persons, and we have learned the health-giving capacity of finding acceptance. But the prestige question is never really solved through loving the self, even when done "properly." Status comes finally, not by seeking it, but by earning it. When power is sought directly, whether by worshiping the devil or by putting in a central place the demoniac goals of wealth or position or prominence, the result is clear. The power drive leads to subservience to the devil. The cost, in terms of divided loyalties, of subjugation of higher standards to lower ones, of overriding of personal relationships in the interest of organizational advancement, is too great.

In the final analysis, as Frankl emphasizes again and again, the power drive is never satisfied directly, but finds its fulfillment as a by-product.[10] Self-esteem grows out of the positive "reflected appraisals" [11] of those who have been helped. This is the answer that Jesus gives to the devil, an answer elaborated on more fully in his later ministry: the position of honor is given to him who serves. (See especially John 13:3-16.) One finds his status through a right relationship with God, a relationship that is testified to in a life of service. The answer given by Jesus makes clear once and for all the major concern: please God, and the status question takes care of itself.

The third temptation, faced both by Jesus and by us, is to evade personal responsibility. More insidious than either of the other two, this temptation has assumed alarming proportions, especially in the American culture which is so thoroughly dominated by psychological and sociological determinism. To be sure, the specific form that the temptation takes for us has little to do with throwing oneself down from the spire of the temple, but the principle is as valid as ever. For us, the particular tendency is to excuse our behavior in the present because of unfortunate childhood trauma or because of an unhappy parental relationship or because of an inadequate amount of loving care.

We have been helped by depth psychology to recognize that the present can be understood only in terms of the past. Our need now, however, is to recognize that the future is not dependent on the past but is rather molded by our conscious decision in the "now." Kierkegaard's admonition is well taken: "Life must be lived forward but understood backward." [12] Gordon Allport writes convincingly of purposeful striving [13] which draws a person toward his chosen goals more effectively than any influences that push from the past. How a person functions autonomously in the present has more to say about the future than do the original beginnings of behavior trends.

Man is responsible for his choices. Indeed, the trait most characteristic of the human being is responsibility. Over and above all conditioning influences, man's life unfolds as he exercises his freedom to make conscious decisions. Jesus would not turn over to God or to his parents or to anyone else the responsibility which rightfully belonged to him. He exercised his human right to accept responsibility for the outcome of his actions, and in so doing he sets the pattern for our lives, too.

The religious world provides a much needed corrective for some of the unhealthy trends rampant today in the therapeutic world. The medical therapist is thoroughly trained to assume personal responsibility for the well-being of his patient, but often little of the responsible attitude toward life is conveyed to the patient. On the whole, the therapeutic world maintains an indifference toward how the patient views his life. Frankl's insistence on the assumption of responsibility for what one is and for what one can become, then, is a welcome change from much of the determinism that the world of therapy has taught, even though often unwittingly. His teaching is in complete accord with the responsible attitude of Jesus.

The need, then, is for a depth psychology to be supplemented with a height psychology that does not discount the dark depths of man's being, but that also recognizes the heights to which he can attain. Without for a moment depreciating the importance of Freud's work in uncovering the demoniac forces that lurk in the unconscious, I would like to assert, along with Frankl, that there is a spiritual unconscious, too, and that man finds his basic orientation for life only as he comes to terms with both of these dimensions. In a conversation with Ludwig Binswanger, Freud is reported to have said: "Yes, the spirit is everything. . . . Mankind has always known that it possesses spirit; I had to show it that there are also instincts." [14] To recognize the importance of Freud's work, especially for his day, is essential, but to see the need for going beyond him for an adequate perspective on life is equally important. Frankl puts it very nicely: Rather than saying that "man is a sublimated animal, we can demonstrate that he conceals within himself a repressed angel." [15]

It is in the atmosphere of a height psychology that the temptations experience comes to an end. How better could the outcome be recorded than to say that "angels came and ministered" (Matthew 4:11b). When fundamental decisions about a life's orientation have been made, when a course has been chosen that keeps one's life open to God and thus to the ultimate values in life, then a sense of quiet contentment fills the heart, as different from the agony of spiritual struggle as are angels from the devil.

II. Mobilizing the Defiant Power of the Human Spirit

Zacchaeus; Luke 19:1-10

Of all the recorded accounts of the encounters of Jesus with people in his day, none is clearer and more detailed than the episode with Zacchaeus. Here is the timeless story of a struggle for status which led to personal alienation and separation from the community. And here is a hint into how the alienated person can be brought back into the community.

In many ways Zacchaeus is far more typical of contemporary man than many of us have recognized. The sense of alienation or isolation has been noted often as an earmark of contemporary city living; one has only to become acquainted with the vast numbers of single persons living alone in a room or two to recognize how prevalent the feeling is. It is commonplace, however, for those of us whose lives are full of positive and meaningful personal relationships to be quite calloused about those whose lives are not so full and who, indeed, crave more intimate contacts. One might think that a theological school residence hall for married students would be a place in which relationships would blossom to full flower, but the fact remains that many a lonely young wife does not dare to take the step or two required to cross a narrow hallway to knock on the door of a neighbor's apartment. Rebuffed so often in hesitant attempts at establishing an intimate relationship, the lonely girl, wanting desperately to be related, nevertheless retreats still farther into her isolation. Wanting to know people and needing their closeness, she nevertheless gives the impression of being distant or unfriendly or unapproachable.

All of us have had some experience with being isolated. Some of us have experienced the kind of isolation created by language barriers. I recall the difficulty my family experienced when I was a boy in Germany, when the German families around us mistook our hesitancy in associating with them for an air of superiority, a mistake which was quickly rectified when they discovered that the problem was largely one of language. In traveling in compartment trains in Europe where six fellow travelers share a compartment, sitting facing each other, it is commonplace to ride for miles without exchanging a word, as if an invisible barrier existed. Indeed, the transformation in the atmosphere created by one who dares to break through the silence by attempting in an awkward, foreign tongue to communicate is marvelous to witness. The more one travels the more he asks himself whether barriers between people are not often due directly to the misunderstandings caused by inability to communicate. Some, indeed, would see mental illness itself as being principally a problem of interpersonal communication.

There are almost no limits to what a person will do to be related. I recall a patient in a mental hospital who, when asked how he was, habitually answered: "I'm better than perfect." His answer generally brought forth a chuckle until one day we were reminded by an astute clinician that the patient was even willing to play the part of a fool if that would evoke some kind of a positive response. Harry Overstreet reminds us that the anguished exclamation of Cain rings true; on being sentenced for the murder of his brother Abel to be a "fugitive and a vagabond on the face of the earth," Cain's cry is: "My punishment is greater than I can bear!" [1] And so it is! To be cut off from one's fellow men is the worst of all punishments. We are beginning to understand that the delinquent or the criminal is often one who has given up in his attempts at relationships on a socially acceptable level. One of my students reported on an inmate in a state prison who presented the picture of the typical hardened criminal: cold, disinterested, unresponsive, sullen. The student, functioning as a chaplain's assistant, refused to be rebuffed by the obvious hostility of the inmate but tried to respond to the man's feelings:

CHAPLAIN: You don't have much desire to have any contact with us and our program.

INMATE: I don't care much to have any contact with anybody.

CHAPLAIN: You are sort of sour on people in general then.

INMATE: That's right! (vehemently)

CHAPLAIN: . . . So, you're going to go it alone now.

INMATE: No, I'm looking for something. I don't know what it is. I have talked with the psychiatrist, he doesn't know what it is either. I feel like I'm up against a brick wall. You know, I've started to come over here to church several times. But I never make it.

CHAPLAIN: Do you feel that there might be something here that would help you?

INMATE: I'm not sure. There is always a chance. I feel like I have to try everything. I would like to feel free to come here to church. I would like it if I could come and talk with the chaplain. I would be glad if I could feel free to come and talk with you.

When the inmate's sullen, resistant manner is perceived as a mask that covers a deep hurt, then the opportunity for change begins to develop. The poet Edwin Markham summarizes the problem, and the solution, very neatly:

> He drew a circle that shut me out—
> Heretic, rebel, a thing to flout.
> But Love and I had the wit to win:
> We drew a circle that took him in! [2]

When Zacchaeus is seen in this light, as a man excluded from relationships, driven into the position of the enemy because of rebuffs in attempts at finding a position for himself within the community, we then begin to sense what that Gospel incident is really all about. To be sure, Zacchaeus is reported to be small in stature; and his climbing a tree is apparently to compensate for his lack of height. But in a far deeper sense he was "up a tree." He could not meet people on the level, in a face to face relationship. He had to put distance between himself and others; he had to stay on the periphery where he could look on without risking the kind of involvement that could lead to the agony of further rejection. There was a good reason for his behavior.

A major contribution of depth psychology has been to point

out that there is a relationship between cause and effect. There is a reason for behavior, and that reason, often hidden at first, can be uncovered. The explanation of cause and effect sequence on both conscious and unconscious levels has added immeasurably to any genuine understanding of man. To recognize, for example, as Harry Stack Sullivan does, that each person develops his own specific "security operation," [3] his own ways of defending his sense of self-esteem and feelings of personal significance, is to begin to appreciate how purposeful otherwise inexplicable action may be. The reason, in the case of Zacchaeus, for assuming the hated position of tax collector, for becoming a servant of the foreign enemy, begins to make sense in the light of the "security operation" concept. If one cannot function in a significant way within his community, if he is driven to feel alienated and isolated from his community, then he will find status in ways that stand over against the community that first rejected him.

It is characteristic of a "security operation" that it tends to reduce the capacity to profit from experience. As Sullivan puts it, one tends to become "selectively inattentive" to anything which threatens his sense of security. Because a security operation is originally seized upon as a protective device, it often becomes an ineffective and inappropriate mode of behavior; yet, because it once served a useful purpose, it tends to reinforce itself as a habitual pattern of behavior and resists evidence that demonstrates its ineffectiveness. One becomes selectively inattentive to opportunities to try anything else. Hence the security operation tends to become more and more the usual method of response. Because the habitual pattern of behavior was originally a defending and protective maneuver, to risk a change is to expose the self, to make one vulnerable to personal hurt. Hence modification of behavior originally chosen as a defensive device becomes increasingly more difficult.

So Zacchaeus, trying to protect a tottering self-esteem, deserted his own people and threw in his lot with the hated conquerors. But he wasn't happy. Caught as he was in his own security operation, he was still hopeful that somehow his situation could be changed. Unable to risk seeking out Jesus about whom his curiosity had been aroused, he could only try to see him from a distance. For the observing person, the undignified position in the tree was a plea for help, but nicely disguised as most pleas are. It is not by happenstance that the colloquial expression "up a tree" has crept into common usage; to be "up a tree" is to be caught in an awkward and embarrassing and somewhat helpless situation.

Zacchaeus, however, did not stay up the tree. The dominant note in this incident centers in change. Regardless of what put Zacchaeus in his predicament, he did not have to stay there. Irrespective of the conditioning influences of his past life, his future life could be and did become different. Great as the contribution of depth psychology has been in the uncovering of the causes that lie behind behavior, it fails as a therapy as long as it focuses attention only on the past. Useful as the concepts of psychoanalysis are for interpreting at least some aspects of behavior, they are often irrelevant when the need is not so much for understanding as it is for change. Another way of putting the issue is to say, as Frankl does, that psychoanalysis does not go far enough.

Having clearly demonstrated that drives do operate in man, the question now is whether drives *determine* man. If the first

29

half of this century can be called the age of psychoanalysis, the second half may well be devoted to a rediscovery of the spiritual. Regardless of what instinctual drives or security operations led Zacchaeus to his unhappy and unpromising situation, the capacity for change was still there.

There is no indication in this account that Zacchaeus gained any insight into the reasons for his behavior; there is clear evidence, however, that a complete change took place in his life. Helpful as intellectual understanding often is, it is by no means determinative, nor is it in any sense a guarantee that any change will follow. More important than the uncovering of unresolved oedipal relationships or the distinguishing of particular security operations or the identification of special defense mechanisms is the conscious decision to confront life as it comes with an optimism about the eventual outcome.

A young resistance fighter, sentenced to death by Hitler's Gestapo, wrote in retrospect of his thoughts in those moments when he stood face to face with death.

One could perceive in that situation how far psychotherapy has yet to go. All orthodox systems break down in comparison with that analysis to which I had to subject myself. Whether this or that indication of psychic imbalance was due to a "complex" derived from a "pregenital," "anal-erotic," or possibly even an "interuterine" trauma; or whether this or that "organ inferiority" was a contributing factor; or whether "archetypes" of my "collective unconscious" somehow entered in—these questions truly were never posed in that situation of waiting for the end.[4]

In critical circumstances any system of conceptualization is less important than the conscious choice of the direction one will take. In the novel *East of Eden*, John Steinbeck underscores the importance of the attitude one takes toward his fate. Based on the biblical story of Cain and Abel, the book is a vivid account of man's struggle to realize his potential in the midst of unfavorable conditioning that seems to bind him to his past. The philosophy of life enunciated by the novelist is expressed in the Hebrew phrase translated "thou mayest." [5] Spoken against a background of perversion and conceit, young Caleb in Steinbeck's novel is given the assurance that he can, if he will, rise above his past even as the biblical Cain was assured that he could rise above his fratricide.

Frankl refers to this capacity of man to rise above the confining restraints of the past with the term the "defiant power of the human spirit."

The spiritual core of a person can take a stand, whether positive or negative, affirming or denying, in the face of his own psychological character structure, as when attempting to overcome a habit or resist an urge. This potentiality essentially inherent in human existence is called in logotherapy the psychonoetic antagonism or the defiant power of the human spirit. What is meant thereby is man's capacity as a spiritual being to resist and brave whatsoever kind of conditioning, whether biological, psychological, or sociological in nature. [6]

This point of view, so basic in Christianity, is one which Frankl reached through wrestling with his own private adversaries.

I had to wrestle but eventually succeeded in building up my own Weltanschauung featured by an unconditional trust in the unconditional meaningfulness of life, which may be phrased by those unconditionally life-affirming words which formed a verse in the song of the inmates of the Buchenwald Concentration Camp and which I chose for the title of a book, *Say "Yes" to Life in Spite of Everything.*[7]

Even Zacchaeus could change. Caught up as he was as a "Quisling," a traitor to his own community, involved as he was in dishonest and underhanded dealings, enmeshed in physical, psychological, and sociological entanglements, he could nevertheless change.

But change never comes easily. Even when one is convinced that the "defiant power of the human spirit" can operate to make basic modification to behavior patterns or in a total life orientation, effecting this change is still a major problem. We have already noted that, like most people, Zacchaeus could not seek help openly. Even at a "teachable moment" when the circumstances were favorable, when he had taken the initiative and had, indeed, even risked ridicule in climbing up a tree, no change would take place unless an atmosphere conducive to change was created. In Markham's terms, even when recognizing the defenses of a "rebel, heretic," how can one "draw a circle" to take the self-established outsider in?

It is from the psychiatric world that we have rediscovered the key to change which is demonstrated so vividly in this encounter of Jesus with Zacchaeus. More important than any theory, more basic than any technique, more significant than any teaching is the one-to-one relationship existing between two people. Whether interpreted in terms of transference and countertransference or of the enhancement of self-esteem through positive reflective appraisals or of more realistic perception of self as reflected and defined by an empathic counselor, the key to change belongs clearly in the quality of a relationship with another person. What makes the relationship effective, over and above the understanding acceptance which is implied in any responsible counseling, is clearly demonstrated in the Zacchaeus incident. Jesus risks himself in such a genuine way that Zacchaeus finds the courage to take the risk of change himself.

It is the philosopher Martin Buber who has contributed the most to our understanding of how interpersonal relationships are related to change in behavior patterns. Distinguishing between manipulating a person as an "it" and relating to him as a "Thou," Buber makes it clear that only as the Thou of the patient relates in a significant way to the Thou of the therapist does real therapy result. Only when the unprotected self of the therapist meets the exposed self of the patient can an encounter that is truly therapeutic take place. Buber comments on the need for the therapist to risk exposure by deserting, on occasions, the protected therapeutic stance:

He has left in a decisive hour . . . the closed room of psychological treatment in which the analyst rules by means of his systematic and methodological superiority and has gone forth with his patient into the air of the world where selfhood is opposed to selfhood.[8]

In a vivid, candid exposure of himself, an anonymous therapist tells of his reaction when an inmate, characterized by a prison social worker as "probably the most hopeless individual I have ever seen," looked the therapist "in the eye and very clearly and slowly said: 'If you give me up, then there is no hope for me.'" The therapist writes of his own reaction.

I was at that moment closer to him than I had ever been to any person on earth. . . . I grew up as it were. I understood that something had been lacking in me, that I was going through motions and following formulas, but that if things got too difficult for me, I was willing to let the lost sheep perish. I also got a glimpse of the importance that I had for him, in terms of a personal relationship.[9]

It was this "critical incident" which proved to be the turning point in leading the therapist to give more of himself and eventually to become the helping person in the complete rehabilitation of the inmate.

The degree to which the helping person must risk himself to penetrate the wall of suspicion and distrust is vividly demonstrated in this incident with Zacchaeus. "Braving" [10] the criticism of the assembled people, Jesus puts himself in the intimate relationship of a guest in the home of Zacchaeus. In this simple act he tosses aside any prerogative of authority and becomes the one who trusts Zacchaeus to take care of his human need for refreshment and his spiritual need for companionship. Totally ignoring the crowd, he demonstrates in this active and specific way his acceptance of the outsider.

The transformation which follows is only the expected outcome of acceptance demonstrated at such great depth. The invitation of Jesus assumed that change could take place. This was acceptance not predicated on change, but acceptance that anticipated change. Acceptance in Christian standards is always of this nature, an acceptance that takes a person where he is but does not leave him there.[11] Seeing a person at his best makes possible his becoming his best. Goethe's maxim, which Frankl likes to quote, states it very clearly: "If we take people as they are, we make them worse. If we treat them as if they were what they ought to be, we help them to become what they are capable of becoming." [12] So Jesus invariably dealt with people.

And so he dealt with Zacchaeus. How the dialogue was carried on in Zacchaeus' home we can never know, but we do know that a dramatic change took place. Whatever was said between the two, the possibility of a change was made clear. Moreover, the promise of reparation for wrongs done makes it clear that the first step toward a change was already taken, the acceptance of personal responsibility for molding patterns of future relationships.

The completeness of the change is implied in the final words of Jesus. Salvation means a new kind of relatedness which includes both the human and the more-than-human. Salvation (or "health" as Tyndale's translation reads) can be complete only when relationships are positive in both the human man-to-man dimension and the more-than-human, man-to-God dimension. No change is genuine until it reaches to all levels, reconciling man not only with his fellow men but with his God as well. Any psychotherapy, therefore, which excludes the higher levels of man's life, his spiritual aspirations and his relationship with God, leaves out a major dimension of life. Thus to speak of the restoring of relationships, of relating an exile to his own community once again in terms of salvation, is to recognize that the spiritual dimension is always present even in man-to-man experiences. Human relatedness is an expression of man's relatedness to God; and man's relationship with God is real only to the degree that it is reflected in man-to-man dealings.[13]

III. Finding the Personal Life Task
The Rich Young Ruler; Mark 10:17-22

The rich young ruler in the Gospel record personifies the contemporary junior executive. Like many men in young maturity in our culture, he had arrived at position and status, had acquired wealth and prestige. But there was something lacking; he found no real pleasure in his life, sensed no real meaning in his existence. He had no clear sense of any personal life task.

The most unhappy persons in our midst are those who lack any sense of involvement in a significant task. Occasional moments of involvement bring a glimpse of possibilities present but often unrealized. Recalling the days of the Berlin airlift in 1948-49, a professional woman declared: "That was the best time of my life." Living in an apartment with no heat during the heart of a bitter cold winter, groping her way through unlighted streets at night, walking through the darkness with no public transportation available, her spirits were nevertheless high. "Hearing the constant, comforting drone of the great American planes flying in supplies overhead," she said, "we West Berliners knew that we had to demonstrate to Russia that our spirits could never be defeated." Of course this was a great period in her life, for here was a time when she felt intimately involved in a meaningful task.

It has been a major insistence of the Christian faith that every person counts, that no person is expendable. For carrying out God's purposes, very ordinary people are depended upon; without their help some of God's plans falter and come to a halt. There is a place in the scheme of things for every single person with his own unique set of aptitudes and abilities and no one else can make the specific contribution that he can make. An opportunity lost by him is lost forever and can never be wholly recaptured. Life has a meaning, and the meaning for every person is found in the fulfilling of a specific life task. The happiest people in our world are those who have found the life task to which they have been called. And the most unhappy are those who have not even begun the search.

The search for a way of life so meaningful that it is worth living eternally is not limited to any one group but is typically characteristic of young maturity, of the man or woman who, having established himself vocationally and having achieved some degree of stability in family relationships and having arrived at some position of prestige in his community then begins to wonder what his life is all about and if the struggle is worthwhile after all. C. G. Jung says that people in this situation who consult him for help commonly express their feeling in the simple words: "I am stuck." [1] As was true of the rich young ruler, wealth and power, often the goals in our culture in the life of young maturity, turn out to be notably inadequate for making life worth living when any real sense of an assignment is missing.

There are a number of reasons for believing that the young man of the Gospel record could be helped. In the first place, he recognized his own need enough to seek help. No well-trained counselor ever underestimates the courage required to present oneself to a counselor with the implied admission: "I have gone as far as I can alone; I need your help." Everyone tries to present himself to others in the best possible light, even to the point of distorting facts and thus obstructing therapeutic progress. But here is a man who had pushed through the initial resistance and asked for help.

Not only did this young man take the initiative, but there is a sense of urgency expressed in impulsive eagerness; how else can one interpret the running up to Jesus and the kneeling before him? Perhaps the man was acting simply on impulse; or perhaps the inner hurt was great enough to lead him to cast caution aside and to forget himself and his position for the moment. Indeed, he may well have felt like a child (cf. the previous passage of Mark 10:13-16), lost in a universe that was not making good sense to him, appearances of wealth and position to the contrary.

Still a third factor created favorable conditions for giving help. This young man seemed ready to accept personal responsibility for his life. He was asking about what he had to do himself. Unlike many who seek help, he was not interested in talking about the unhappy circumstances of his early life, or the unfortunate conditions that surrounded him, or the difficult people that he lived with. In a responsible way he seemed ready to take action to remedy a pattern of life which was bringing material success but no genuine satisfaction.

The key to the handling of this man's problem is found in the first words which were spoken by Jesus. Jesus lifts the whole encounter into another dimension. Whereas the young man sought an answer in terms of acts he would perform, presumably in terms of ritualistic practice such as attending church, giving a tithe, and reading the Scriptures, or in terms of doing good and avoiding evil, Jesus implies a much more basic God-centered orientation in which every aspect of life is open to spiritual values. Whereas an answer to personal problems might be sought in terms of personal dynamics (uncovering unconscious driving impulses) or of interpersonal relationships (resolving personal antagonisms or reducing barriers in social relationships), Jesus raises the question of the adequacy of the young man's frame of reference and points to the need for considering the dimension of life that is concerned with ultimate meanings and values.

Implied here is a recognition that more and more workers in therapy are coming to, that any therapy which does not take account of questions dealing with values and meanings is simply not adequate for our day. Viktor Frankl takes vigorous exception to Freud's point of view in this matter. Freud once wrote in a letter to Princess Bonaparte: "The moment a man questions the meaning and value of life, he is sick." [2] Frankl comments on these words by saying: "I think, on the contrary, that such a man only proves that he is truly a human being." [3] Frankl notes that at least three dimensions of reality need to be distinguished: the somatic or organic, the psychic or psychological, and the noetic or spiritual.[4] Because most psychotherapies stay in either the somatic or the psychic realm, they do not really treat the whole man.

Indeed, the uniquely human aspect of man is to be found neither in the soma nor in the psyche but in the spirit. The spiritual dimension designated by Frankl as the "noetic" indicates the deciding, responsible aspect of man. It is man's responsibleness which distinguishes him from the animal. It is the stress on the noetic (i.e., the spiritual but not necessarily the religious) [5] that is a major contribution of logotherapy. As Frankl puts it:

Logotherapy deviates from psychoanalysis insofar as it considers man as a being whose main concern consists in fulfilling a meaning and in actualizing values, rather than in the mere gratification and satisfaction of drives and instincts, the mere reconciliation of the conflicting claims of id, ego and superego, or mere adaptation and adjustment to the society and environment. [6]

In a similar way, Gordon Allport notes that the human being "pursues certain biological goals; but he also pursues other goals which require him to establish his own identity, to take responsibility, to satisfy his curiosity concerning the meaning of life." [7]

From another perspective the world of values is seen as a necessary dimension in life. C. G. Jung, in describing the circumstances that lead to the common dilemma of middle life, [8] that of being "stuck," notes that the tendency in our culture is to develop only one aspect of a person's life to the almost total exclusion of the other. Like the rich young ruler, most men in our western culture stress the aggressive, action-oriented "masculine" side of their nature in getting started in a career, in establishing a family, in acquiring possessions, to the almost total exclusion of the more philosophical, meaning-oriented "feminine" side of their lives. In the prime of life, however, when the early struggles are over, the unlived aspect of life seeks expression. When the unlived aspect of life cannot find expression it becomes destructive. In a similar way, logotherapy asserts that when life oriented to meaning does not find expression, it becomes destructive, leading to the sense of disillusionment and discontent which is so common in middle-age.

It should be noted that a similar problem often exists for the woman, but in a reverse pattern. Whereas her early years of adult life are generally devoted to the care of children, thus accentuating her feminine role, middle-age brings her the felt-need for a more aggressive ("masculine") participation in life. Much of the conflict of marriage in middle life can be understood in terms of these patterns, for at the very moment that the wife desires to assert herself more to play a larger role in affairs outside the home, her husband is turning from a life of active involvement and is looking in the direction of less active, more contemplative pursuit of a meaningful philosophy of life. At any rate, the major point that Jung makes is that any complete life is a well-rounded one that makes concerns for values and meaning as significant as any other aspect of life. No counseling can be adequate that does not include a careful consideration of the counselee's value orientation.

To be sure, Jesus did refer to a specific code, to the standards for moral conduct which have proved to be the very basis of social living. His reference, however, was first to God, to a God-centered life, to a life oriented around supreme values. The commandments become, then, an expression of the relationship to

God (cf. Matt. 5:23-24) rather than simply the rules for personal conduct, rules which the young man had so scrupulously followed. He knew the rules, but he had no real sense of involvement in a personal life task. Like Oscar Hammerstein, who found the inspiration for the lively opening chorus in the musical "Oklahoma" in the lifeless stage directions printed in the margin of a script of a play, the rich young ruler needed to put the stultified words of the commandments into the broader harmony of a meaning-centered life.

To make such a change, however, was more than this young man could manage. Unlike Jesus, who had already resolved that immediate things were secondary to long-term values, this man's life had been so built on the acquisition of things that people and relationships with them had been crowded out. Reuel Howe puts the issue very concisely: "God created persons to be loved and things to be used." [9] Whenever this order is reversed so that things are loved and people are used, tragedy results. One of the commonest values to be derived from psychotherapeutic sessions is often related to these concerns. In the life of an attractive young matron, the turning point in counseling came when she recognized that her seductive and promiscuous flirting with men had been her way of manipulating them as things rather than really relating to them as persons. In a similar vein a psychiatrist colleague once told of how his therapy group with psychotic women was at a deadlock until he made it clear to them that his interest in them was not as feminine objects to be exploited but as people to be helped. Indeed, it is a common experience in working with disturbed people to find that resistance to forming relationships is almost insurmountable. It is as if their psychic energy is so tied up in maintaining protective defenses that none is left for going out toward others.

If any change were to be made, Jesus adopted the one pathway likely to effect it. "Jesus looking upon him loved him." The key is found here not only to the personal ministry of Jesus, but, indeed, to any effective ministry. Here is represented what Sullivan speaks of as the "quiet miracle of developing the capacity of love." [10] Sullivan's reference in particular is to the preadolescent era when a youngster gains a feeling of personal significance through positive "reflected appraisals," through seeing in the eyes of his chum that he counts. The implications hold true, however, for the entire range of human relationships. The first impulse to change comes not so much from being challenged as by being loved. It is only in an atmosphere of loving acceptance that barriers to relationships can be lowered. As one young wife once put it: "My husband tells me that if I loved him I would keep the house picked up. How can I help him to see that the only way I can find the strength to pick up the house is through the absolute assurance that he loves me whether the house is tidy or not?" First the assurance in the look of love, then the challenge.

Note, however, that the challenge is there. There is little that is nondirective in the ministry of Jesus.[11] The imperative could hardly be more direct: "Go! Sell! Give! Come! Follow!" When the counselor is dealing with a lack of purpose, he has to provide active help in discovering the purpose. His task at this point is twofold: on the one hand he has to help the counselee to sense that life is worth living, that it does have a meaning; on the other hand he has to help the counselee to find the specific personal meaning that beckons, that awaits fulfillment. In both these tasks active participation is called for.

It is important to note that the counselor, himself, does not assign a task to his counselee. Rather he assists the counselee in uncovering the assignment which is already there but which has not been fully recognized. So, for example, in a concentration camp Frankl helped two comrades who were close to suicide, because they expected nothing more from life, by enabling them to view their lives in a new perspective; one found meaning in the child that waited to be cared for, and the other reformulated his goals in terms of a series of books that awaited his completion.[12] Frankl uses provocative questions to evoke an awareness of personal meaning when nothing worthwhile seems to remain. He tells of dealing in a therapy group with a woman whose son had died suddenly, leaving her with another son who was crippled and paralyzed. She was in rebellion against her fate largely because she could see no meaning in it.

When joining the group and sharing the discussion I improvised by inviting another woman to imagine that she was eighty years of age, lying on her deathbed and looking back to a life full of social success but childless; then I asked her to express what she would feel in this situation. Now, let us hear the direct expression of the experience evoked in her—I quote from a tape: "I married a millionaire. I had an easy life full of wealth. I lived it up. I flirted with men. But now I am eighty. I have no children. Actually, my life has been a failure." And now I invited the mother of the handicapped son to do the same. Her response was the following—again I am quoting the tape: "I would look back peacefully, for I could say to myself, 'I wished to have children and my wish was granted. I have done my best, I have done the best for my son. Even though crippled, even though helpless, he is my boy. I know that my life is not a failure. I have reared my son and cared for him—otherwise he would have to go into an institution. I have made a fuller life possible for this my son.'" [13]

Just as the therapist helped the sorrowing mother to see personal meaning in her life, so Jesus directed the young man to the task that awaited fulfillment by him, the use of his unique talents not to accumulate more riches but to enrich the lives of men through more intimate personal relationships.

The Christian faith has always asserted that God plays an active role in man's life. There is a sense in which God provides an assignment for each person in life. Rather than asking what the meaning in life is, the more appropriate question is to ask what task God has in store for any one individual. [14] "In what way can I, being the person I am, with the unique set of talents and experiences that I have, fulfill the tasks that are waiting for me to undertake in God's world?"

There is a final note in the account of the rich young ruler that indicates how well Jesus understood the difficulty of the challenge he had set forth. He offers his own constant support by proposing that the young man throw in his lot with the disciples. [15] Presenting a task that would arouse obvious tensions, Jesus offers personal support to help in the struggle. So indeed, a fellowship of support is needed for risking the chance of failure that is always present when old ways are dropped and a new direction is taken. It is not enough, then, to present the challenge for finding the personal meaning in life; it is not enough for an informed counselor to present the challenge in the accepting milieu of understanding love. A fellowship of accepting people is also needed, a fellowship that will stand by as hesitant and stumbling attempts are made to break away from meaningless routine and to explore more meaningful patterns of relationships.

Sometimes the counselor fails. Sometimes the patterns are too firmly entrenched to yield to any approach, no matter how persuasive. It is the very nature of man that he is free to say "no," just as he is free to say "yes." But the counselor does not despair, for even as the seeker turns away sorrowfully, he has been exposed once again to the assertion of the fundamental worthwhileness of life and to the possibility of involvement in it in a very personal way.

IV. Filling the Existential Vacuum
The Samaritan Woman; John 4:4-27

The story of the Samaritan woman at the well is the story of any person whose life is characterized by an inner emptiness, by a spiritual vacuum. A major contribution of Frankl is his insistence that the most fundamental human need is to fill this emptiness, to find a personal meaning for life. All of the needs, whether the need for satisfying hunger or for gratifying the sex drive, or for achieving status, or for attaining power are secondary to the basic search for meaning.

The capacity of man to endure hardships when he has a firm grasp on the meaning of life is quite limitless. During the years which he spent in concentration camps, Frankl observed that the ones who could not survive the rigors of the camp life were often those who had lost all sense of any meaning in life. "The prisoner who had lost faith in the future—his future—was doomed." [1] Nietzsche's statement underscores Frankl's conviction: "He who has a *why* to live for can bear with almost any *how*." [2]

In the more common experiences of life, too, it is clear that the finding of meaning gives a reason for living. Frankl tells of an elderly general practitioner who was in a deep depression for two years following the loss of his dearly beloved wife. By reminding him that his wife had been spared the kind of suffering he was going through, the old doctor was given a new perspective on his suffering. "In that very moment," Frankl writes, "his mourning had been given a meaning—the meaning of sacrifice. The depression was overcome." [3]

Much longevity can be ascribed to a strong sense of meaning in life. The great German poet Goethe lived just two months beyond the completion of the second half of his masterpiece, *Faust*, dying at eighty-three. Writing of him, Frankl notes: "I dare say that the final seven years of his life he biologically lived beyond his means. His death was overdue but he lived up to the moment in which his work was completed and meaning fulfilled." [4] Most of us are acquainted with the sudden physical deterioration that can set in on an apparently healthy man as soon as he retires. Without work, without the meaning that having a job to do provides, there is hardly any point in continuing to exist.

To be sure, secondary goals do, on occasion, become the primary ones. Hunger, for example, can become the all-consuming need. But Frankl points out that such a secondary goal functions in a primary fashion only where the search for meaning has been lost sight of or has been given up. Refuting Freud's insistence that under conditions of starvation, the one unsatisfied instinct of hunger takes precedence over everything else, Frankl notes: "In the concentration camps we witnessed the contrary; we saw how, faced with the identical situation, one man degenerated while another attained virtual saintliness." [5] It is where the search for meaning has been abandoned so that a vacuum exists that secondary goals become primary ones. In an attempt to fill the vacuum, goals that are inappropriate for man take priority. Such was the situation with the Samaritan woman at Jacob's Well.

The Samaritan woman presents a vivid picture of what Frankl calls an "existential vacuum." The meaningless, monotonous routine of her life is expressed graphically in the spontaneous cry which came from her after Jesus had penetrated through her outer defenses: "Give me water, that I may not thirst, nor come here to draw." The more precise meaning of the Greek text might be rendered as follows: "Give me this water that I need not keep coming in this dreary drudgery, day after day, to draw water in the meaningless routine of everyday existence." The ritual of daily tasks held nothing but weariness for her because she had lost any sense of meaning in her life.

Any contemporary psychological counselor can testify to how common this experience of an existential vacuum really is. In an astute observation, psychologist Edith Weisskopf-Joelson notes that the usual psychoanalytic classification has no clear place for "existential vacuum." She observes that in Freud's day neurotic patterns fell into rather clear-cut categories: hysteria (converting emotional problems into physical symptoms), obsessions and compulsions (being obsessed with an idea or feeling compelled to perform a specific act), and phobias (inappropriate and groundless fears); today, however, the commonest symptoms fall into none of these syndromes but are characterized instead by a sense of emptiness, a feeling of meaninglessness, by a treadmill quality in daily life and by a fuzziness about values.[6]

It is to be noted, as Frankl does, that this sense of being lost in the universe is not a sickness in a pathological (i.e., abnormal) sense. Existential vacuum does not describe an illness so much as a condition that is often present where there is no pathology at all. To be sure, existential vacuum may also exist where there is acute illness, and in such cases must be recognized and treated along with other symptoms that are more abnormal. But for the most part, the sense of aimlessness in life is a characteristic of those who are physically and mentally well but spiritually sick. To refuse to recognize the existential vacuum for what it really is, a loss of the sense of meaning, and to try to treat it without reference to the world of values, is to fall into the common fallacy of psychologism which sees value concerns only as secondary defense mechanisms rather than as primary legitimate conscious concerns.[7] One of Frankl's patients volunteered on one occasion how her interest in the spiritual life had been scoffed at by therapists over the years:

Why is it that I feel ashamed about all religious things, that they appear embarrassing and laughable to me? Well, I know exactly why I am ashamed of my religious needs. The basic emphasis of psychological treatment as I have experienced it for 27 years from other doctors and clinics, has always been that such spiritual longings are old-maidish, foolish speculations; for only that which one sees and hears is important, and everything else is nonsense, created by traumas, or is only a flight into sickness (in order to evade life). So when I spoke of my need for God, I had to fear that by doing so the straight-jacket would be brought to me. Every kind of treatment until now has always missed the mark.[8]

It is notable that Jesus dealt with the Samaritan woman in terms of the value conflict in her life. The brief and obviously telescoped account of the incident does not make it clear how Jesus knew about the woman's marital entanglements, but a clear hint is given in the fact that she sought water by herself at about noon (the time corresponding to the Hebrew sixth hour) rather than joining the other women of the town at the usual early morning period of sociability. To miss the usual exchanges of friendly gossip seems to indicate a serious rupture in her relationship with the women of the town. To this issue Jesus directed his attention with forthright directness.

It would be quite possible to excuse this woman's way of life in terms of early conditioning forces or of insurmountable economic and social factors. Our culture readily finds an explanation for behavior in psychological or sociological conditioning. The fact of the matter, however, is that to deal with conditioning factors is to deal with only one part of the picture, albeit a very important and necessary part. The decisive factor does not lie in the conditions; the determining element is found in personal response to the conditions. "Freedom," as Frankl puts it, "is freedom to take a stand toward conditions, but it is not a freedom from conditions." [9] Man is responsible for how he handles the conditions which life presents to him.

The directness with which Jesus confronted the Samaritan woman with her immorality reminds us that some human problems are simply the result of irresponsible action and are not to be explained away by psychodynamic interpretations. Great as the contribution of depth psychology has been to our deeper understanding of forces at work beneath the surface in man, we are in danger of overlooking the most human aspect of life, if we fail to hold man as accountable and responsible for his action in the present and in the future. Conscious decision with a definite goal in mind can break the circle of behavior dictated by past conditioning. Indeed, even within the psychoanalytic world a new stress is being given to ego-psychology in which the ego is conceived not merely as an umpire among conflicting instinctual forces but as an executive directing behavior forward into the future. Life can be pulled by goals, as Frankl phrases it, just as surely as it can be pushed by drives.

But the goals need to be adequate ones. To indicate to this woman the futility of finding happiness sought through the doorway of sexual pleasure was a major emphasis in Jesus' ministry to her. Recognizing that she had tried to fill the existential vacuum with the pursuit of pleasure, Jesus did not hesitate to make an issue of the matter. If he could help her, like the prodigal son, to come to herself, she could be helped to see that self-realization through pleasure seeking is invariably a dead-end street. Over and over again in his ministry Jesus underscored the folly of making as an ultimate goal that which is only a by-product of more significant goals. Pleasure comes, not by seeking it, but by finding the satisfactions of filling one's responsible place in life.[10] In the significant study of "creativity" now being carried on at the University of California, a tentative finding is that the most creative person turns out to be closer to the prototype of the responsible professional person than to that of a San Francisco beatnik.[11]

The reaction of the Samaritan woman to being confronted with the moral problem in her life is highly instructive. Her first reaction was to change the subject with a bit of flattery thrown in. Religious discussions are often a way of avoiding real involvement on a personal plane. Most study groups conducted under religious resources that fail are failures not because of a lack of vital material to deal with but because the material is so commonly unrelated to immediate personal life situations. The Samaritan woman's reference to the appropriate place for worship, although a timely question, was in reality a "red herring" designed to interest the religious leader but to divert the conversation to a safe, impersonal level. The continuation of the conversation into the debatable question about the coming of the Messiah only demonstrated how hard it was for her to look at herself. Indeed, from the beginning she had been on the defensive, throwing up a barrier even in the presence of a simple request for help in getting a drink of water. So defensive was she that she could not even accept a friendly overture but felt compelled to be suspicious and restrained, to fall back onto the prejudices of the day.

But Jesus was not taken in by her defensiveness. He recognized it for what it was, an uncertainty fostered by the unresolved moral issue that plagued her life, a protective barrier behind which she could hide her private unacceptable behavior. Unlike the kind of response to which she was accustomed, he did not respond defensively. He accepted her and her defensiveness without retaliating in kind. He refused to reject her as she rejected him; but he refused, also, to allow her to dictate the terms of their relationship. Refusing to move away from her and her predicament, he nevertheless took the topic of conversation offered to him, redirected it into an area of personal relevance for her, and related her need to the larger dimension that included God. The implication was very clear; the only way to the kind of life that held real meaning for her ("living water") was to clear up the moral problem which made impossible a true relationship either with her fellow human beings or with God.

Jesus did not hesitate to confront this woman very directly with her problem. It was not his practice to evade difficult issues. His very presence in Samaria made this clear, for whereas other Jews often chose to avoid Samaria by roundabout detours, he chose to go straight through on his journey from Judea to Galilee. The King James translation uses picturesque words to describe the event: "He must needs go through Samaria." Being the kind of person that he was, he "must needs" confront her. Note, however, that the real confrontation was made only when she had invited a serious discussion about her predicament.

A refusal to ignore the kind of immoral relationship that is destructive of real, loving relationships is recognized as good procedure in any competent counseling. An acceptance of destructive behavior is only "pseudo-permissiveness" [12] and actually works against the best interests of the counselee. The reaction of the Samaritan woman rings true. Rather than rejecting the confrontation made by Jesus, she acclaimed his deep understanding of her life situation, even forgetting to complete her original errand of drawing water in her distress at the new hard look which she was compelled to give to herself. Her invitation to others to talk with Jesus is the best possible proof of the effectiveness of his ministry to her. She wanted help in getting to the rest of the meaninglessness in her life. She needed help in learning that life, directed to different goals, could become meaningful.

V. Resolving Value Conflicts

The Paralyzed Youth; Mark 2:2-12

The power which can be exercised over the physical organism by feelings of guilt is well illustrated in the story of the young man with the paralyzed legs. Long before the advent of psychosomatic medicine, the Hebrew writers had recognized the essential unity of body, mind, and spirit and had stressed the relative dependence of one upon the other. When Jesus approached this man as one whose primary need was for the assurance of forgiveness, he was reflecting the Jewish thinking of his day that sin and health are related,[1] but in a larger sense he was demonstrating a recognition of the relationship which exists between attitudes of the mind and health of the body. Carroll Wise reminds us of how this approach of Jesus has been confirmed by modern medicine: "Physicians have discovered that guilt, like anxiety, may serve to inhibit or paralyze the functions of the body or mind." [2]

Apparently Jesus recognized that the paralyzed youth was

struggling with moral conflicts, and that the struggle had resulted in guilt feelings which he could not handle. It is important to note that Jesus took the moral issue seriously. A common error in contemporary life has been to see all conflicts centering in moral standards as derivative from something else, to refuse to take moral problems seriously. So a serviceman, wounded by a self-inflicted injury, is treated not in terms of his internal moral conflict but in terms of unresolved oedipal problems, and a young father seeking help in marital discord is treated without any concern for his strong sense of commitment to the marriage vows. Indeed, one of the most insidious dangers in psychoanalytic ways of thinking is that along with the profound wisdom growing out of the study of unconscious motivation there is a corresponding blindness to the presence of realistic, conscious, moral issues. To study, for example, the great spiritual leaders of the world's history in terms only of past conditioning without any reference to the decisive part played by conscious commitment is to read only one half of the story, and, indeed the less important half.[3]

The fact is that unresolved moral issues not only lead to the pursuit of compensatory secondary goals, as in the case of the Samaritan woman considered above, but they may also lead to actual illness. The turning point in the therapy of a sexually promiscuous young woman came when the therapist dropped his investigation of background motivation and simply forbade his patient to continue her self-destructive, exploitive pattern.[4] Until her direct violation of her own moral code had been dealt with the therapy was at a standstill. In another case, reported by a minister,[5] a young woman became gradually paralyzed following an accident, even though two successful surgical procedures had given her full use of her legs. Filled with hateful feelings toward her parents, and feeling very guilty because of the hate, she was literally paralyzed by her emotions. When the minister saw her first, she did not believe that God would ever forgive her because of her breaking of the commandment to "honor" her parents. When the minister, in the process of counseling, helped her to accept the forgiveness of God, and eventually to become more accepting and forgiving of her parents' failings, the paralysis disappeared completely.

It is in the light of such situations that we can understand the account of the healing of the young paralytic brought into the presence of Jesus by four friends. Mark's account with its familiar address ("My son"),[6] leads us to believe that the man may have been an adolescent boy caught up in some of the moral and psychological conflicts so common in many adolescents. At least, we see in him a young person who was asking some profound questions about life and his place in it, and was not finding clear answers. Some of the questions must certainly have centered around his sense of failure to measure up to his own standards. Who knows but what, like the woman with the paralyzed legs, he, too, may not have resolved the common problems of effecting independence from his parents without a strong sense of guilt.

It is quite normal for young people to struggle with questions about the meaning of life, and it is not uncommon to find some who, like the paralyzed boy, are incapacitated by the struggle. In treating a seventeen-year-old girl afflicted with what was diagnosed as an incapacitating heart disease, Dr. Frankl discovered that he was really dealing with an adolescent girl struggling with a conflict of values. When he indicated more interest in her spiritual longings than in her heart ailments, she talked eagerly and in considerable detail about this area of her life. She complained of her inability to find the meaning in life, told of the occurrence of some mystical experiences within her own religious life, and indicated her longing for knowing final truth in rational terms. Her predicament was complicated by an unsympathetic boy friend whose interests were openly epicurean and who ridiculed her assertion that the pursuit of pleasure was an inadequate goal.

In working with this girl, Frankl recognized that the heart symptoms were a reflection of her disturbed state of mind in the presence of many unresolved questions. He began therapy by noting that the asking of questions about the meaning of life is in no sense a sickness but is, on the contrary, a distinguishing mark of being human:

Who searches for meaning? Certainly an ant will not, neither will a bee. A girl, however, of 17, posing such questions and involved in such a quest proves to be a truly human being struggling for meaning. . . . You are right in contending that pleasure cannot be the main thing in life. Struggling for a meaning in life, at the risk of foundering in the search with questions and even doubts, is not only normal during puberty but is even the prerogative of youth. A truly young person never takes meaning for granted but dares to challenge it.[7]

Continuing, Frankl asserted that spiritual maturation often leads to periods of distress but that such distress is to be conceived of as an expression of growth, of spiritual becoming, and not to be confused with mental illness. He made no objection to her mystical religious experiences, noting that her contemplative withdrawal was not at the expense of social interests but was rather an indicator of the normal upreach of her spirit, reminding her that "if trees stand near to each other and cannot grow in breadth, they grow in height." He saw her restless search as being typical of the historic quest for God immortalized by St. Augustine's words: "Our heart is restless until it finds its rest in Thee." [8]

In this approach, Frankl was following the direction taken by Jesus in working with the young paralytic. The boy was approached not in terms of his paralyzed legs but on the level of his spiritual problems. We are not in a position to know in detail just what his problems were, but we do know that the concern of Jesus was not for the symptoms but for the young man's total attitude toward life. Torn apart by a sense of sin, perhaps precipitated by adolescent feelings of guilt, this young man needed Jesus' reassurance of God's forgiveness of his sins. Only when he was clear in his own mind about his acceptability in spite of his sins was he freed from the paralyzed state and, with encouragement, was able to resume a more normal life at home. His preoccupation with himself, his self-reflection and consequent self-reproach were set aside so that he was no longer bound up in indecision or immobilized in self-doubt.

It has already been noted that Frankl gives a special meaning to the word "spiritual," and that he designates this meaning by the word "noetic." If the noetic realm is perceived as the decision-making, value-oriented dimension in human life, and if the noetic aspect of life is conceived of as being at least as significant as any other area, then conflicts can be expected in the noetic dimension just as they can be expected in the psychological realm. That is, neurosis can be noögenic (from the noetic) just as clearly as they can be psychogenic (from the psychological). In this sense logotherapy is not so much a "height" psychology, but, more accurately, is a "wholistic" psychology. As for the young man healed by Jesus, it is quite likely that he was totally unaware of how his spiritual unconscious was leading to his somatic problem. It took the discerning eye of Jesus to sense the moral problem and thus to clear the way for physical recovery.

There are other details of the story which clarify how the young man was helped. The limits to which his friends went to make help available could not have failed to make an impression on him. When four friends were concerned enough about him to carry him to the presence of one who might heal him, and when they refused to be deterred from this goal by the presence of a crowd but improvised an approach on the spot, tearing open the roof and lowering the boy into the very presence of the visiting teacher, the dramatic effect could not have been lost on the boy. Obviously the four friends thought him worth helping even to the point of exposing themselves to the wrath of the homeowner and the displeasure of the crowd.

Karen Horney, who wrote so helpfully about the common emotional problems of living, described three characteristics of a therapeutic situation [9] which are nicely illustrated here. The first is an atmosphere of warmth; this was clearly indicated in the presence of the four friends. Horney points out how an atmosphere of warmth is essential for the fulfillment of one's own potential. The freedom for a person to be himself is dependent upon his feeling accepted in his uniqueness. We are reminded here of Sullivan's concept of reflected appraisals referred to earlier. Certainly the support of loyal friends helped the young man to feel that, in spite of his shortcomings, he was worth something. In a very real way the friends set the stage for the events that followed. *Their* faith quickened *his*.

The second aspect of the therapeutic situation which makes change possible, as noted by Horney, is the guiding encouragement of a significant person (or persons) of goodwill; this was provided in our story by Jesus. It often takes a counselor or therapist to fulfill this role, especially when life conditions have been severe and loving relationships conspicuously absent. But Horney is optimistic about what normal, healthy associations can do even for seriously disturbed people.

Analysis is not the only way to resolve inner conflicts. Life itself still remains a very effective therapist. Experience of any one of a number of kinds may be sufficiently telling to bring about personality changes. It may be the inspiring example of a truly great person; it may be a common tragedy which by bringing the neurotic in close touch with others takes him out of his egocentric isolation; it may be association with persons so congenial that manipulating or avoiding them appears less necessary.[10]

There is still a third characteristic of a growth-inducing climate, indicated by Horney, which is not as obvious as the other two, but which may actually be the decisive factor. Horney speaks of it as a "healthy friction with the wishes and wills of others." Another way of putting it is in terms of challenge, the setting of a goal to work toward. People are helped not just by acceptance, essential though this is; they are helped, too, by a challenge to move out from the protective atmosphere of acceptance to forge their own pathways. Jesus put the challenge very bluntly: "Take up your bed and walk!" The implications are quite clear: "It's all right to have friction. It is not sinful to resist your parents. Go home. Go back to your family. You can handle your problem." [11]

Frankl never tires of setting the challenge. When treating the seventeen-year-old girl referred to earlier, he moved from asserting the appropriateness of her spiritual struggle to challenge her to discover the personal meaning that life held for her. When she asserted that she believed there is a meaning to life, but that she didn't know how to find it for herself, he declared:

Man finds the meaning of his life not so much by reflecting on it as by committing himself to the immediate challenge of the concrete situation. Dedicate yourself to the here and now, to the given situation and the present hour, and the meaning will dawn on you. Try to be honest to yourself in pondering your vocational possibilities as well as your personal relationships. I would do injustice to you and to your freedom of choice if I took over any decisions like these. They are up to you and therefore you should keep in mind your responsibleness. Struggling for a meaning in your life, for a life task, may be the immediate task of your present life. [12]

When she insisted on wanting a rational explanation for the meaning of her daily tasks, Frankl asserted that it is a mark of maturity to be able to endure the struggle without clear-cut answers.

If you cannot grasp it intellectually, then you must believe in it emotionally. As long as I haven't found the supra-meaning but have only an inkling about it, I cannot wait until I am 80 years of age and only then dedicate myself to it, but must rely on my vague inkling and commit my heart in serving it. And this holds for God who is the warrant for the existence of supra-meaning, as mankind has developed the concept throughout history. Self-commitment and fulfillment of life's concrete challenge is the road at the end of which we are awaited by wisdom so that ultimate meaning becomes intelligible. This intellectual achievement is preceded by existential commitment. Trust in the wisdom of your heart, a wisdom which is deeper than the insight of your brain! [18]

Under this therapeutic approach, the girl made a complete recovery.

The evidence from such contemporary cases where permanent recovery follows the patient's changed attitude toward himself and his place in life leads to the belief that where spiritual (noetic) problems are actually confronted and dealt with, the consequences in terms of physical health can be quite amazing. It is very clear that the ministry of Jesus included physical healing; it is now becoming clear how spiritual problems and organic disability may be related. In any event, Jesus was primarily interested in restoring man's relationship with the supra-human world, and in doing so clarified man's unique place in his own human environment. When the challenge to realize hidden potential is given in an atmosphere of understanding acceptance, and when the challenge is given with a guiding hand that helps to make the way clear, then transformations as amazing as the healing of the paralyzed youth can be expected.

VI. Actualizing the Self in Responsible Commitment

Simon the Pharisee; Luke 7:36-50

Simon the Pharisee is a good illustration of a man who had never really come to terms with himself. Complacent in his own self-righteousness, he saw no need in his own life for forgiveness, and hence, as the parable in this incident stresses, knew little about love. Jesus put the matter very succinctly: "He who is forgiven little, loves little." Committed as Simon was to self-realization through a literal obedience to the religious law, he was too busy pursuing his own righteous way to really make room in his life for others. Neither Jesus nor the woman who had been a sinner were given more than passing attention, as he was engaged in self-fulfillment through the law.

There is, to be sure, a school of thought which declares self-fulfillment to be the goal of man's existence, and there is a sense in which this is true. The happiest persons are those who have realized their potentialities. We have already seen how unlived life, how undeveloped capacities, can become destructive.

We recognize the validity of the position that stresses making the most of the abilities with which one has been endowed, and subscribe to the point of view that the development of a many-sided personality is one of the best ways for getting the most out of life. The most creative personalities of our age have been those who have been able to come to terms with all that is within their makeup and to bind together the several different aspects of their personalities into a meaningful whole.[1]

A good deal of emphasis in the therapeutic world is devoted to unravelling the knotted strands that make for inner conflict and hence prevent self-realization. There is a good deal to be said in favor of the homeostasis principle, the principle of satisfying the conflicting claims of id, ego, and superego so that the personality is not torn apart by inward strife but is rather able to function without undue internal discord. When Sullivan talks of euphoria as the goal of life, he is referring to such a tensionless state in which the ego, presumably, is free to move out into any chosen direction without being held back by unresolved personal problems or unmet neurotic needs. The peace of mind concept has the same goal of eliminating the anxieties that keep the personality torn apart and unable to move in any sense.

It is doubtful, however, if such tensionless states are ever possible even if they were desirable. The pursuit of a tensionless existence, like the pursuit of happiness, turns out to be an impossible goal. Peace of mind does not come by searching for it; like happiness, it comes "on-account-of" something else. It is the by-product of meaningful activity rather than a legitimate goal in itself.[2] Indeed, the most complete sense of peace of mind is generally experienced only after the successful completion of a task, a task which oriented the worker away from himself and onto something greater than himself. Real peace of mind comes not from a tensionless situation but rather from the completion of a tension-creating task. Contrary to much popular thought, the tensionless state of ease and pleasure leads more often to the frustration of an existential vacuum than it does to any real peace of mind.

In a similar way, self-fulfillment or self-actualization, as a goal in itself, is seldom achieved. Frankl notes that "neurotic straining after 'happiness' in love leads, precisely because of the strain involved, to 'unhappiness.'" In like manner, self-realization is seldom achieved when it is sought directly; like happiness, self-realization comes in the fullest measure as a by-product.[3] A person realizes his fullest potentiality when he commits himself to a task great enough to call upon all of his talents and abilities. Like the mother who finds strength to accomplish amazing feats when her child's life is in danger, under the compelling power of a worthwhile goal one uncovers unexpected ability and at the same time realizes something of one's potential. It was this aspect of life that was so largely lost sight of by Simon the Pharisee.

Simon, like the Pharisees he represented, was a good man in the commonly accepted sense of the word. Indeed, in his rigid keeping of the law, he was such a good man that he had no sympathy with others who were less strict in their religious observance. His very preoccupation with his own morality, made an end in itself, blinded him to the kind of goal that could have helped him really to fulfill his own potentialities. Preoccupied in his attempts to avoid sinning himself, he had no sympathy with those who were not as strong as he. His unspoken but obvious condemnation of the woman who was a sinner betrayed a basic discontent in his own life, a discontent that grew out of a lack of relatedness with people. His predicament was later the predicament of Saul of Tarsus who found the way out of a similar plight only by a complete reversal of his way of life.

The problem that Simon faced is the problem that anyone faces when he becomes engrossed in self-reflection. Preoccupation with one's progress, heightened sensitivity to how one is doing, thwarts the very progress desired. Consider, for example, how focusing attention on going to sleep makes sleep quite unlikely, or how a determination to stay awake makes sleep more probable. Or note how the artist, who is too much aware of the artistic production he is creating, finds that his self-consciousness stands in the way of his best performance.[4]

Frankl points out that many sexual neuroses have their origin in hyperattention or in hyperintention. The man who feels compelled to carry through the sex act is often rendered impotent by the very hyperintention; and the woman who attempts to compel herself to experience an orgasm is the one least likely to do so. He reports on a woman who, in complaining of being frigid, cited a conditioning background of sexual abuse and consequent anticipation of difficulty.

When she had her first sexual experience she began to observe herself during the sex act because of her apprehensions. Thus neither her attention nor her affection was directed toward her partner, but her goal was to experience an orgasm "at last" and thus to confirm her femininity. The feeling of pleasure of the orgasm, which normally follows automatically, was thus made a specific goal. This by itself is enough to frustrate the orgasm, but it is even more the case when pleasure is not only the object of intention but the object of attention as well.[5]

When this woman's excessive attention and excessive intention had been deflected away from orgasm and refocused on her partner where it rightfully belonged (i.e., "dereflection" in Frankl's terminology), no further difficulty was experienced.

Contrary to Simon's distorted perception, man's primary concern does not lie in his personal fulfillment. Far more important than self-actualization is the finding of a personal meaning in life, a point of reference which is outside of one's own personal existence. Frankl puts it very clearly: "Man's primary concern does not lie in the actualization of his self but in the realization of values and in the fulfillment of meaning potentialities which are to be found in the world rather than within himself or within his own psyche as a closed system." [6] The feeling of real fulfillment comes not by more strenuous efforts at self-actualization, but by more meaningful contact with the objective, external world.[7] And this contact with the outside world is understood best in terms of personal responsibility.

We have already noted that a disciplined sense of responsibility is a marked characteristic of the most creative personalities. It is the sense of responsibility that puts the mark of greatness on the spiritual leaders of any age. When David was King in Israel, he often fell into temptation, but his redeeming grace was that he kept the tension tight between what he did and what he ought to do. Even in weakness he did not lose sight of his responsibility. The "ought," the most characteristically human aspect of his makeup, was never completely covered over. And it is because the "ought" has an outward reference away from the self to the area of relationships that it is so important. Rather than lessening the sense of obligation, in a life that is weak, the "ought" needs to be given more attention, like the weak arch that is strengthened by the architect by adding to the load it carries.[8] Man's life is to be understood not in terms of pressures of the "I must" (psychological or sociological) that push him in unconscious ways, or of the "I can" which suggest self-actualization as a possible goal, but rather of the "I ought" which relate man to the external world of value.[9] It was the lack of the sense of personal obligation and personal responsibility for others that Jesus condemned so specifically, not only in Simon but in the Pharisees as a whole.

The road to personal maturity, leading as it does away from excessive attention to self-actualization and toward commitment with a clear sense of moral responsibility is referred to helpfully by Gordon Allport. In discussing religious maturity in his book *The Individual and His Religion*,[10] he speaks of three specific avenues along which a person must travel. It was in directions such as these that Jesus habitually worked, as is illustrated in his approach to Simon.

The first avenue that Allport refers to is the avenue of self-objectification or of self-detachment. Since self-detachment is difficult for anyone and almost impossible for a person like Simon who was so caught up in his own concerns, Jesus chose to use a parable in which Simon could see himself more clearly through identification with characters in the story. Like David when confronted by the prophet Nathan with a similar parable (II-Sam. 12), Simon placed himself on record, committed himself to a position, only to discover that he had then passed judgment on himself.

If self-objectification were easy, most of the problems of personal relationships could be cleared up with relative ease. Indeed, a major reason for the development of therapeutic groups is that in the group the members are helped to see themselves as others see them through free discussion of behavior as it takes place. Jesus made use of the group situation, calling both himself and Mary to Simon's attention and noting the difference in the courtesies extended by Mary in contrast to Simon. Here was irrefutable evidence that helped in self-objectification.

Allport notes that self-detachment is often accomplished through humor. Humor, at its best, is the capacity to laugh at oneself. It is always the sign of strength when individuals, or governments, can laugh over the jokes made to ridicule them. A major technique in logotherapy is the use of humor through belittling symptoms; by making light of his symptoms a patient establishes distance between himself and them.[11]

The avenue of widening interests is Allport's second point, an emphasis already touched upon in the concept of refocusing. It is not enough to simply deflect attention away from the self; a new area of concern needs to be found. As was characteristic of Jesus, he not only dealt with Simon's problem of self-interest, but he also pointed to the woman who had been a sinner as a more appropriate concern. The implication in his question: "Do you see this woman?" is that Simon had never really seen her as a person but had dismissed her as one of the category of "sinner." By pointing to Simon's failure to feel any responsibility for his own needs, Jesus further attempted to widen the focus of interest.

Frankl makes major use of the principle of widening interests. In writing of a nurse who was in despair because her illness prevented her from carrying out the work in which she had found so much fulfillment, he reports:

I tried to help her to understand that to work eight hours or ten hours or God knows how many hours a day is no great thing. Many people can do that. But to be as eager to work as she was and to be incapable of working yet not despairing would be an achievement few could attain. And then I asked her, "Are you not really being unfair to all those thousands of sick people to whom you have dedicated your life as a nurse? Are you not being unfair if you now act as if the life of a sick or incurable person—that is to say, of someone incapable of working—were without meaning?" I said, "If you despair in your situation, then you are behaving as if the meaning of our life consisted in being able to work so and so many hours a day, but in so doing you take away from all sick and incurable people the right to life and the justification for their existence." [12]

In working with senior citizens in the over sixty-five group it is commonplace to discover that all kinds of illnesses quickly fill the vacuum of empty hours after retirement unless new interests are discovered or old interests are reactivated. In the Christian faith the concept of commitment has always been central. One finds his life, not by holding on to it, not by jealously guarding it, but rather by giving it freely, by losing it in the interest of others. And the paradox spoken by Jesus inevitably is proved true: "Whoever would save his life will lose it, and whoever loses his life for my sake will find it" (Matt. 16:25).

Allport's third avenue refers to an integrating principle around which one can build his life, a principle which provides a new coordinating center. The condemnation which Simon's behavior called forth was not because he was not a good man so much as it was that his pattern of life stood in the way of attaining more important values. The context within which he lived his life was not large enough. He felt a keen sense of responsibility for the conduct of his own life, but he failed completely to feel any sense of responsibility in areas that were not a part of his own narrow world. His preoccupation with the moral law cut him off from real contact with most of his fellow men.

This account of Simon and the sinful woman recalls the story in John's Gospel (John 8:2-11) of the woman who was caught in the act of committing adultery and whose death through stoning, according to the law, was averted only by the quiet intervention of Jesus. Here, too, a sense of responsibility to the religious law had blinded the men concerned to a responsibility to a fellow human sinner. Here, too, the interest of a preoccupation with self-realization had taken priority over any sense of responsibility toward more ultimate values.

It is this concern for more ultimate values that characterizes Frankl's logotherapy. The most distinctive aspect of logotherapy lies in its insistence on a personal responsibility that means far more than the development of self-potential; it is a sense of responsibility that recognizes different kinds of values and chooses a relationship with the highest values. In this emphasis Frankl underscores the characteristic approach of Jesus.

There is no better passage than this account of Simon's encounter with Jesus for seeing the typical method with which Jesus approached the Pharisees. The record in other places is quite clear that open denunciation was directed at the pharisaical way of life: "Woe to you, scribes and Pharisees, hypocrites! for you cleanse the outside of the cup and of the plate, but inside they are full of extortion and rapacity!" (Matt. 23:25). However, this encounter with Simon is more consistent with the general tenor of Jesus' ministry. He used the immediate, current circumstance to point out the problem in Simon's life, kindly but firmly confronting Simon with the facts of his behavior. First allowing Simon to pass sentence on himself, Jesus then drove home his point. And to the sinful woman both in Simon's house and in the temple square, his words were the same: "Your repentance cleanses you from the past. Go in power into the future, no longer faced with the compulsion to sin but freed to live a responsible and committed life."

VII. Realizing Creative Values
Peter; Matthew 16:13-19;
Luke 22:31-34, 54-62

The story of Simon Peter is the story of a dramatic transformation; it is effective testimony to the impact made by Jesus on a man. But even more specifically, it demonstrates the change that can take place when a meaningful cause takes over a man's life. From the start of the record, Peter is depicted as a well-meaning but bungling fellow whose intentions are always good but whose impulsive declarations seldom materialize into effective action. Whatever one makes of Peter's attempts at walking on the water (Matt. 14:25-33), or of his attempted defense of Jesus in the Garden of Gethsemane (John 18:10-11), he is portrayed as a man of quick emotion whose heart is in the right place but whose actions are often inappropriate. Quick to affirm his loyalty, his threefold denial that he even knew Jesus, although he had been forewarned, was typical of his instability when the pressure was on. Yet Peter became the spokesman for the disciples, was the leading member of the inner circle of

Jesus' closest associates, and was the recognized leader after the death of Jesus (Acts 1–5).

The transformation in Peter's life can be understood principally in terms of the mission which he undertook to carry out. The threefold admonition to "feed my sheep" as recorded in John 21:4-19 underscores the sense of purpose which motivated him after the death of Jesus. His failures in the past counted as nothing in the presence of the tasks that waited fulfillment through his hands. It is as if the admonition of Jesus in his first recorded contact with Peter became the central concern in Peter's life: "Launch out into the deep" (Luke 5:4 KJV). His mission "in the name of Jesus" gave direction and stability to his life; from a man of weakness he became a man of strength.

It is Frankl's central thesis that life is transformed when a mission worth carrying out is uncovered. Moreover, it is Frankl's assertion that everyone has such a mission, such a life task waiting for him. In talking with a young artist on the verge of a complete schizophrenic break he declared to her, calling her by name:

> You cannot reconstruct your life without a goal in life, confronting and challenging you. . . . Isn't there a goal, an artistic assignment beckoning you? Are there not many things fermenting in you, unformed artistic works, undrawn drawings waiting for their creation, waiting to be produced by you?
>
> Let's think of the fact that you are Hildegard and that there are things which wait for Hildegard—unborn works of artistry. . . . They are your creations and if you don't create them, they will remain forever uncreated.[1]

This attitude which Frankl advocates is one which does not ask what can be expected from life but asks, instead, what life expects of a man. Speaking of his experiences in the concentration camps Frankl writes:

We needed to stop asking about the meaning of life, and instead to think of ourselves as those who were being questioned by life—daily and hourly. Our answer must consist, not in talk and meditation, but in right action and right conduct. Life ultimately means taking the responsibility to find the right answers to its problems and to fulfill the tasks which it constantly sets for each individual.[2]

Peter's experience with Jesus is a good illustration of how one man was helped to take the responsibility for finding deeper meaning in life than he had hitherto recognized.

We have already noted that, for Frankl, finding a meaning for life is man's principal task. It is in specifying how meaning can be found that Frankl makes a major contribution. He describes three principal ways in which meaning in a personal sense can be found: through realizing creative, experiential, and attitudinal values.

We are particularly interested for the moment in the first: creative values.[3] Meaning in one's personal life is most readily realized through the act of creativity, of active involvement in life with the goal of contributing through personal accomplishment. Who has not known the satisfaction of a job well done, or the relief that comes from the completion of an assignment? And who has not experienced the depression that closes in when there is no job to be done, no assignment to be tackled, no task to call forth unused potential? Frankl tells of how the desire to publish the basic formulation of logotherapy helped to give meaning to his life in the years of concentration camp experiences. He had lost the completed manuscript at the time of entering the Auschwitz camp, but in the course of imprisonment he was able to rewrite the major outline, partially by using shorthand. When confined to his bed with typhus fever, while running a high temperature, he jotted down his notes on the back of mimeographed forms stolen for him, along with the stub of a pencil, by one of his comrades. He says that in spite of the raging fever his thoughts were crystal clear, and the work that eventually resulted was little changed from the outline formulated then.[4]

It is a commonplace experience to discover, as Frankl did, that sickness does not prevent the completion of creative tasks. Many an artist can testify to the disappearance of even disabling physical symptoms when engaged in creative, artistic performance. The physical organism seems to function at its best when its energies are devoted to the accomplishment of a task, and fatigue goes unnoticed until the task is finished. A well-known conductor of the Vienna Philharmonic Orchestra, Bruno Walter, reports in his *Memoirs* that although he was troubled by severe pains in his arms, the pain disappeared while he was conducting.[5] Harvey Cushing, Boston's distinguished brain surgeon, wrote at eighty: "The only way to endure life is always to have a task to complete." [6] Frankl notes that he had never seen "such a mountain of books on anyone's desk all waiting to be read, as on that of the 90-year-old Viennese Professor of Psychiatry, Joseph Berze." [7] He was too busy to die! Indeed, the sickness of depression frequently turns out to be the sickness that results from a failure to see any creative task to fulfill. A painter, contemplating suicide, tells of how his eye fell upon a painting that needed to be amended just as he had turned on the gas. Seeing work waiting for him to finish, he forgot his suicidal intent and went to work to finish the painting.[8]

The hard fact, however, is that some never seem to be able to get started in finding creative tasks to give themselves to. Caught up in the comfortable patterns of familiar though often meaningless routine, many never launch out into the adventures which can lead to a genuine sense of meaning in life. Some remain resigned to be passive spectators when active involvement is a real possibility. Some simply watch television from an easy chair while real life passes by on the street outside. Some remain fishermen when they might become fishers of men.

It is clear that accepting the responsibility to perform life's tasks, to realize creative values, often calls for an intermediary step; there is often the need for someone to put the challenge! It is very clear that Jesus saw his ministry in these terms. He was constantly presenting the people whom he touched with a challenge. Sometimes the challenge was only implied in the manner described by the playwright in "The Passing of 'Third Floor Back,'" [9] the play in which an unknown roomer in the back room on the third floor of a run-down rooming house so touches the life of all the other roomers that their best selves are called forth in a way that makes a radical change in their lives. More often, at least in the record as transmitted, Jesus set the challenge in pointed ways: "Go! Sell! Give! Come! Follow!" For Simon Peter the challenge was at once an affirmation and a hope: "Blessed are you, Simon Bar-Jona [Son of Jona]; . . . you are Peter [that is to say a rock, from the Greek *Petros*]" (Matt. 16: 17-18).

It was Harry Stack Sullivan who emphasized the role played by self-esteem. For him, until a person's self-esteem had been made secure, little else could take place, and certainly no change. Sullivan made it a cardinal point to make certain that his treatment procedure never undercut a person's sense of self-esteem, and most counselors attempt to follow in his steps. Indeed, it seems likely that before many a person is in a position even to consider a challenge, he needs to feel supported as a person of significance. Certainly this is one of the things that was happening in the relationship of Jesus and Peter.

Peter's initial sense of unworthiness is vividly described in the record. Note, for example, the words he uttered in the initial recorded contact with Jesus: "Depart from me, for I am a sinful man, O Lord" (Luke 5:8). And consider the vivid scene in the courtyard of the high priest's house where Peter denied knowing Jesus three times, each time with greater vigor as prompted by an uneasy conscience; then, catching Jesus' eye, he heard the cock crow, realized what he had done, and "went out and wept bitterly." But Peter discovered that failure was not the last word. Even though he could not undo the act of denial, he could redeem his past by changing himself. He could never erase the fact of failure in the moment of crisis, but he could atone for the failure by becoming a changed man. He could detach himself, as Frankl says, from his deed by growing away from it morally.[10] Real repentance is indicated by a changed life. That Peter did change is made very clear in the subsequent story of the early Christian church. That he had been helped to climb above failure is equally clear.

To learn to live with failure is one of the marks of maturity. Instead of being devastated by failure, the mature person profits from his mistakes and moves away from them, not requiring of himself that he always succeed. A student in a summer training program in a clinical setting had learned a significant lesson when he could summarize his learning experience with the words: "I can dare to fail." Freed from the necessity of always succeeding, no longer required to achieve every goal set forth, he was released from the confines of the narrow road of absolute certainty. No longer was he restricted to those patterns which had been tested and of which he was sure. He could now adventure into the unknown, not certain of the outcome but able to tolerate the possibility of failure. Failure no longer loomed as an intolerable possibility, and by this very fact its likelihood was lessened. No longer striving only for success, with the self-imposed tension of required success gone, a successful achievement was more likely.

Many in our day are confused about the requirements of success. Taught by our culture that "anything worth doing is worth doing well," many are easily trapped into the conclusion that the only permissible outcome is a successful one. Even though this demand for success seldom has any objective validity, even though it is seldom imposed by anyone, it nevertheless operates in many lives with deadly effectiveness. One astute observer notes that many persons tend to become their own worst parents, tending to put requirements upon themselves which are far greater than those imposed by their real parents.[11] They tend to require of themselves that they demonstrate their worth through successful achievement. And so they dare not fail!

It was characteristic of Jesus that the emotional support which he gave so freely was always honest in its appraisal and candid in its frankness. He never felt impelled to soften the facts in the interest of supporting a sagging self-esteem. Knowing Peter's temperament, he called attention to how easy it was to make assertions of loyalty when carrying them out would be quite a different matter. Indeed, it was this very quality of candor which helped his words of challenge, when they were uttered, to carry weight. His typical relationship was not clouded over with well-meaning but untrue assurances; people know where they stood with him.

It is universally true that effective personal relationships must be open and honest. Not only was it important for Jesus to speak openly to Peter of too-easy professions of loyalty; it was also desirable that their relationship be free enough for obvious displeasure to be expressed. When Jesus was critical of the sleepy Peter, who could not stay awake on watch during his personal crisis in the Garden of Gethsemane, he could speak about it freely. This kind of freedom demonstrated by Jesus in so many of his relationships is being stressed in many current writings as a major key in counseling. Paul Tournier writes of the importance of a freedom in human relationships that permits an open expression of genuine feeling.

I saw that by adopting a more personal tone myself I was helping others to become personal, not only in my consulting-room, bu in the most ordinary conversation in the street, on military service, or in a medical conference. And I realized how men thirst for this real contact, from which new life springs up to blow like a fresh breeze among us and within us.[12]

Frankl is another contemporary exponent of the kind of freedom that Jesus demonstrated. He speaks of the need for the neurologist to put away his reflex hammer in order to encounter his patient as "man to man, I to Thou." [13] Frankl is one of the commentators in the book *Critical Incidents in Psychotherapy*, a book which develops the thesis that the turning point in therapy in some thirty cases seemed to come when the therapists ventured into the realm of unabashed, spontaneous emotional involvement. One of the therapists tries to explain the change which followed an angry outburst on his part: "Before I had been a kind of official, interested in doing a job, but not interested in Homer. After, because of my anger, I became a person, and one who was interested in him." [14] Frankl comments on a similar case in this book:

> The aggressiveness of the therapist serves to indicate his willingness to meet the patient on a man-to-man level, putting himself on the same level as the patient. . . . It proved to the patient that he was considered seriously, as a person accountable for his action—in other words, as a person who should be ready to take responsibility.[15]

To be sure, the relationship of Jesus to Peter (and, indeed, to all whom he touched intimately) was more than just outspoken openness. The really supportive aspect of it was the acceptance that was present, regardless of how Peter acted. The look that passed between the two in the courtyard of the high priest would be hard to describe, but it was certainly the look of understanding acceptance and not the look of rejection. Indeed, the record seems to indicate that it was out of the understanding acceptance of Jesus that Peter was able to measure up to the challenge of leadership; first the acceptance, and then the change. And so the helping ministry continually proceeds. Change comes out of challenge, to be sure, but the challenge is invariably rooted in acceptance.

It goes without saying that the basic change which took place in Peter's life turned him from a reliance upon personal resources to a reliance upon powers far greater than his own. Beside the greatness of his task, his own human failings became unimportant. Personal failure counted not at all; the success of the mission to which he had been called became all-important. Accepted as one who could accomplish the tasks set before him, and empowered by the challenge of the task, he became a far stronger man than he had even hoped to dream of. Accepted as he was, he risked change to become the man he was capable of becoming.

VIII. Realizing Experiential Values
Mary and Martha; Luke 10:38-42

The differing approaches to hospitality shown by Mary
and Martha demonstrate not only two basic attitudes toward
life but also present graphically the dilemma of the contemporary
American woman. The incident, moreover, brief as it is, gives
considerable insight into the effectiveness of the ministry of Jesus.
Paul Tillich helps us to recognize the significance of these few
verses when he writes that "the words Jesus speaks to Martha
belong to the most famous of all the words in the Bible." [1]

A part of the appeal of this incident comes from the sympathy
commonly felt for Martha. No matter what the needs of the
hour were, some routine tasks had to be fulfilled. Someone had
to prepare the meal. Martha's irritation seems pretty natural,
and her spontaneous outburst is quite understandable. Why
should she have had to do all the work while her sister sat back
like a lady of leisure? From her perspective her complaint was

entirely in order, and she must have fully expected that Jesus would support her.

But Jesus didn't. On the contrary, he used Martha's demand as an opportunity to try to help her to understand herself better. He was not manipulated by her complaint, legitimate though it may have seemed to be, into hasty condemnation of Mary. Indeed, the only word of criticism which he uttered was in the nature of an observation of what Martha was doing herself. "You are anxious and troubled about many things." It is as if he were saying: "Instead of being critical of Mary's behavior, look more closely into your own." As Jesus well understood, work can become feverish activity to cover over a meaningless life. It can be used as a demand for love rather than as an expression of love. Carroll Wise reminds us that "in some relationships the self is so threatened that he feels he must bolster himself in all relationships by activity. His activity is an endeavor to secure the love of others, and like Martha, he becomes resentful if this love is not forthcoming." [2] It is not enough simply to be working; the motive behind the work is important, too. Indeed, it is significant that the Mary and Martha incident follows the parable of the Good Samaritan, as if to say that service itself does not tell the whole story of life.

Jesus did not intend to belittle the importance of the area of creative accomplishment. He did mean to indicate that this is not the only area of life in which meaning can be found and, indeed, to suggest that Mary was finding meaning on an even more significant level. In terms of the American woman of today, it could be said of Mary that she refused to be cast into the commonly accepted cultural role of homemaker. She insisted on being a person and not only a woman; she refused to fit into the stereotype which has been characterized as the "feminine mystique."

The term "feminine mystique" has been coined by the writer Betty Friedan and used as the title for a penetrating, thought-provoking book. She documents in careful detail the forces that have led the contemporary American woman away from full participation in the world of creative ideas and meaningful action and back into a domestic scene centered around the family hearth. "Why," Betty Friedan exclaims, "should she [the American woman] accept this new image which insists she is not a person but a 'woman,' by definition barred from the freedom of human existence and a voice in human destiny?" [3] When one housewife describes her predicament of household routine for her family of three children, the overtones of Martha's condition, "anxious and troubled about many things," come through:

By noon I'm ready for a padded cell. Very little of what I've done has been really necessary or important. Outside pressures lash me through the day. Yet I look upon myself as one of the more relaxed housewives in the neighborhood. Many of my friends are even more frantic.[4]

It was this pattern of frantic limiting activity that Mary was rejecting, and it was her choice of another pattern that offered more in the way of real self-fulfillment that Jesus was supporting.

A major contribution of logotherapy is its insistence that meaning in one's personal existence cannot be limited to one narrow area. Thus, for example, the woman who is denied the experience of being a mother is unrealistic if she thereby feels that her life is no longer worthwhile. And the man whose vocational placement gives him no satisfaction is likewise unrealistic if he expects to derive meaning only from his job. When obvious values are denied, then meaning needs to be sought in other ways, on other levels. We have already noted the three levels of creative, experiential, and attitudinal values which logotherapy distinguishes. Our particular interest here is in the second level. Creative values, although the commonest, are only one way of finding meaning in life. Values may also be realized in experiential ways.

In experiencing something or in encountering someone, experiential values are actualized. Such values might be realized, for example, by "surrendering to the glory of an experience" as, for example, when one is "sitting in a street car [and] . . . has opportunity to watch a wonderful sunset, or to breathe in the rich scent of flowering acacias." [5] Frankl discusses a therapeutic interview with a sixty-one-year-old ornamental painter whose progressing neurological disease made it impossible for him to continue the work which he loved. "Unwittingly I focussed on experiential values since there was no longer access to creative values. . . . I tried to evoke his thankfulness for his past professional achievements, his present valuable artistic experiences, and his good marital life." [6] The interview centered on the intellectual pursuits which this humble man was pursuing, the university extension courses he was taking, the works of Gorki and Dostoevski which he was reading. Frankl reinforced the painter in his conviction that there was still meaning in life even without the broader areas of the familiar tasks of manual work.

Even more significant than experiencing something, however, is encountering someone. The "good portion" which Mary chose was the "one thing needful"—a personal encounter. As Mary sat at the feet of Jesus and listened to his teachings, we can sense how important this must have been for him. The incident takes place shortly after the record indicates that "he set his face to go to Jerusalem" (Luke 9:51b), facing the inevitable crisis which would lead to his death. However much he needed food for the nourishment of the physical man, the deeper need was certainly for a responsive listener with whom he could discuss the deepest concerns of his heart.

It is from Carl Rogers and "client-centered therapy" that we have learned of the significance of listening. Rogers believes that communication breaks down because people do not really listen and hence do not really hear what is being said. As words and concepts are screened through private experiences and prejudices they become so distorted that they carry little of the meaning originally intended. Rogers recommends that any response be preceded by an attempt at restatement so that before the response is given, the listener makes sure that he is responding to what was really meant. It is commonplace in marriage counseling to discover that husband and wife are talking together without really communicating, and that what is heard is not what is intended at all. I have watched members of therapy groups completely misinterpret comments so that an attempt at personal support has been perceived as a direct attack or a clumsy try at personal sharing has been understood as personal antagonism. Listening is hard, but real listening makes for real encounter.

Of course, Mary did more than listen. She made Jesus' concerns her concerns. She entered into his world with him. She found meaning for her own life, as she related herself to the concerns of another. It is in this perspective that Frankl reports on a man who was overwhelmed by a sense of weariness with life until he found a girl in a similar situation: "When he met a girl in the same straights and saw in her his task of comforting her over her weariness of life—at the same instant his own experience had finally taken on a meaning once more." [7]

In Frankl's own life, creative and experiential values tend to be combined as he enters with empathy into the interests and needs of his patients and finds renewed meaning for his own life. While he was in a concentration camp, shortly before its liberation, he had an opportunity to escape and, indeed, had made his plans to do so until one of his patients asked him in a tired voice: "You, too, are getting out?" Frankl reports the uncomfortable feeling which came over him, and then his sudden decision:

Suddenly I decided to take fate into my own hands for once. I ran out of the hut and told my friend that I could not go with him. As soon as . . . I had made up my mind to stay with my patients, the unhappy feeling left me. I did not know what the following days would bring, but I had gained an inward peace that I had never experienced before. I returned to the hut, sat down on the boards at my countryman's feet and tried to comfort him. [8]

We have already indicated that there is no single way to realize values, and that different circumstances call for different approaches. It is obvious, however, that some ways are preferable to others, and that some values are more important than others. The familiar "love" passage of I Corinthians 13 is understood in its full impact only when the last verse of chapter 12 is read with it: "And I will show you a still more excellent way. If I speak in the tongues of men and of angels, but have not love, I am a noisy gong or a clanging cymbal." [9] Not that there may not be value in spiritual gifts which express themselves in strange tongues, but that there *is* a more excellent way, the way of relationships with people so understanding and accepting and forgiving that it becomes transforming. Among concerns that are good, some are better than others. Important as home and family concerns may be, they are not the only concerns in life. It is to this point that the story of Martha and Mary speaks.

In commenting on this story Paul Tillich uses the phrase "the ultimate concern." [10] The phrase is a choice one. Among many concerns which are good, the discovery of the most important, the ultimate, is a highly significant task. Jesus' gentle rebuke to Martha is not because she is wrong in her activity, but because she is less right than Mary is. Mary has put the priority where it rightfully belongs—on personal relationships. She sees *encounters* as more important than *achievements;* she values people over things. Unlike the rich young ruler who had so built his life on things that he could not extricate himself, Mary had established a basic priority that she would not give up even though it created tension with her sister.

To the credit of Martha, it should be said that creative values *are* essential for life. Indeed, there are some who would say of experiential values, that the most meaningful kinds of personal encounters come best in a common pursuit of a worthwhile task. There is no doubt that the ministers and laymen working side by side on the island of Iona in the task of putting together a place of worship, stone by stone, feel a comradeship that penetrates to depths seldom reached in mere discussion; or that the American men in alternative service who rebuilt with their hands the Karlschule in Vienna, wrecked by bombs from their own land, were experiencing a bond of fellowship in common manual labor pointed toward a worthy goal that surpassed most of the superficial personal relationships of the past. Indeed, there is even reason for declaring that the choicest kind of constructive "togetherness" comes, even in a classroom, as alert minds move together in the pursuit of a clearer formulation of truth. The point is, however, that when the task is the major goal, the persons involved are easily lost sight of.

The mild rebuke to Martha, then, is in order, not because her service as hostess is unimportant, but because it can be a block to relationships at a deeper level. The prosaic tasks of routine, everyday family living obviously have to get done; the danger is that they become ends in themselves. There is no emphasis more basic in Jesus' ministry than the stress on the priority of personal relationships. With graphic effectiveness the story of the Prodigal Son, for example, reaches its climax when the younger brother "came to himself" and reappraised his life in terms of personal relationships rather than in terms of things that could be used for pleasure. The criticism that Jesus leveled most often against the Pharisees was that their keeping of the law, good as it was in itself, had become a barrier to a relationship of justice and mercy with other people.

It is unlikely that Martha changed her role under the instruction of Jesus; such habit patterns do not lend themselves easily to change. But at least she must have sensed that Mary was performing a service, too, even though expressed in a very different way. Activist that she was, Martha could easily miss the kind of encounter at the deeper level in which soul meets soul, and so the support that Jesus gave to Mary was in order. Without discounting the pathway of creative values, he made it clear that experiencing another person was on an even higher level.

IX. Realizing Attitudinal Values
The Bethesda Invalid; John 5:2-15

The healing of the Bethesda invalid is a story with many facets, but its central significance lies in a fresh approach to illness. Whereas in our culture the tendency is to focus on the symptoms in illness, Jesus put the major stress on the attitude taken toward the illness. The essence of health, as Jesus saw it, had less to do with an absence of symptoms (as our culture tends to define it) than with an inner state of wholeness out of which physical health emerged. This inner state of mind is independent of organic conditions and is not dependent on an absence of suffering. Indeed suffering, itself, may contribute to an inner sense of wholeness and peace. Whereas our culture tends to avoid suffering at almost any cost, the New Testament faith, developing as it did out of the crucifixion followed by the resurrection, insists that something very redemptive can emerge out of suffering.

There is a sense in which suffering is just as much a part

of life as is pleasure. Indeed, rightly understood, suffering contributes far more to life than does pleasure. Walt Whitman has a poem in which he speaks of the contribution of resisting forces in life:

> Have you learned lessons only of those who admired you,
>   and were tender with you, and stood aside for you?
> Have you not learned great lessons from those who braced
>   themselves against you, and disputed the passage
>   with you? [1]

It is in a similar vein that Robert Browning writes:

> Then, welcome each rebuff
> That turns earth's smoothness rough,
> Each sting that bids nor sit nor stand but go! [2]

Frankl, too, gives a large place to suffering. Like Jung, he sees the attempt at avoiding suffering as being a sort of neurotic pattern. Frankl writes:

> Suffering and trouble belong to life as much as fate and death. None of these can be subtracted from life without destroying its meaning. To subtract trouble, death, fate, and suffering from life would mean stripping life of its form and shape. Only under the hammer blows of fate, in the white heat of suffering, does life gain shape and form. [3]

In the conviction that suffering belongs to life and can be used creatively to discover meaning in life, Frankl underscores the conviction of Jesus. The Christian faith has always been concerned with the elimination of human suffering, as innumerable hospitals erected under Christian auspices all over the world indicate, but the condition of physical health is only a part of the concern. The larger concern centers less in symptoms than it does in attitudes. In a similar way Frankl's approach is one that looks more at the attitude than at conditions. This is especially true with regard to physical symptoms. The tendency in medical circles is to so focus attention on the symptom that the underlying attitude is lost sight of. It is the assertion of logotherapy, however, that many symptoms (although, obviously, not all) are the direct result of unhealthy attitude, and that often relief can be accomplished by changing the attitude rather than by treating the symptom. In this sense the question asked by Jesus to the Bethesda invalid is quite in order: "Do you want to be healed?" The implied question is, "How do you look on your illness? How does your illness affect your attitude toward life?"

The question of Jesus directed attention not to the man's illness but rather to his outlook. Whereas the invalid talked in terms of the help that others never gave to him with the result that he had lost hope, Jesus puts the stress on his attitude about himself. Concerned for so long with how others could help him, the invalid had overlooked how he might help himself.

It is to be noted that in so focusing attention on the attitude and away from the symptom, attention is directed to the future rather than to the past. The implication is that whatever the conditions have been in the past that caused the symptoms, the important factor is not so much the uncovering of an underlying conflict responsible for the symptom as it is the adoption of an attitude which makes possible a handling of the symptom. Whereas the commonest emphasis in the therapeutic world today seems to be on investigating the relationship between causal factors and symptomatic expression, logotherapy questions the necessity for always finding the cause in the past and stresses the importance of working with the attitudes in the present; [4] logotherapy finds that many a symptom disappears when the attitude is changed. Consider, for example, the case treated by Dr. Frankl of a mother with several young children who became gradually immobilized by a phobia of bacteria. The case notes read as follows:

She no longer left her home lest she contract infection. She did not allow any visitors to enter the home, for she was afraid they might smuggle in a disease. She had no servant nor any help, for nobody was clean enough. Many hundreds of times daily she washed her hands. She completely withdrew into one small room in her home where even her children and the members of her family were not allowed to enter. Throughout these years her husband was not allowed to touch any of the children. She finally wanted a divorce because she felt she had made her family unhappy and that she ought to free them from such a burden.

Eventual suicidal attempts led to her hospitalization. In treating her, Dr. Frankl helped her to make her fears ridiculous by exaggerating them. Paradoxically, he encouraged her to intend what she had feared:

Then I started "paradoxical intention." I invited the patient to imitate what I did before the whole audience (a class). I scrubbed the floor of the lecture hall with my hands and said thereby: "After all, for the sake of a change, now let us not fear but wish to be infected. I cannot become dirty enough, not enough bacteria." [5]

Responding to Dr. Frankl, the patient began to rub her hands on the floor, and then, following his example, on her face. As the ridiculousness of the situation struck her, she began to smile, and with the smile her change in attitude began. In five days, with repeated instruction and practice in "paradoxical intention," ninety per cent of her obsessions and compulsions disappeared even though she had been ill for three years.

It is important to note that when attention is focused on attitudes, then there is never a situation which cannot be helped in some way. Frankl likes to quote Goethe's saying: "There is no predicament that we cannot ennoble either by doing or by enduring." [6] It is Frankl's conviction that he can always give *some* help to anyone who comes to his clinic. "Everybody can be helped, if not directly by psychoanalytic approaches, then indirectly by helping the patient to change his attitude." [7] This was certainly the mood in which Jesus confronted the Bethesda invalid. Even though the man had been ill for thirty-eight years, there was no reason for believing that his situation, or his attitude, could not be changed.

It is rather clear that, by himself, this man had been unable to effect any change in his life. Like most people, he saw the limiting conditions that surrounded him rather than the creative possibilities. Health, for him, meant only recovery from the crippling physical symptoms. Yet there must have been something about him that singled him out from the others who were there. The one hint that the story gives us suggests that he was still trying. It is quite conceivable that Jesus picked him from the crowd because he hadn't given up; apparently he had not settled completely for the secondary gains of illness. At least the question of Jesus opened up the whole subject of the meaning for him of his illness.

Illness is not without its compensations. Some, actually, do not want to be healed. It is quite possible that the Bethesda invalid had settled into a fairly interesting and perhaps even profitable vocation, the vocation of illness in which he was the recipient of considerable sympathy and attention.[8] I recall a man who was thoroughly enjoying a self-assigned task of research in a public library as a result of the fact that a fear of crossing any street made gainful employment apparently impossible. He resented, strongly, any efforts at resolving his problem (and, of course, compelling him to go to work). His answer to the question of Jesus, at least unconsciously, was: "No, I do not want to be healed." The fact of the matter was that he had lost the courage to handle his life and so had retreated into illness. He was defeated by life. His real need was for help in mobilizing the defiant power of the human spirit; he needed help in daring to believe that he could find meaning by facing life rather than by withdrawing from active involvement into passive illness.

One of Frankl's major contributions lies in his assertion that meaning in life can be found in the very attitude that is taken toward suffering. Ordinarily meaning is found in daily life through creative activity or through experiencing something or someone, but when these pathways are closed, the way of handling suffering is still open. Meaning is thus found not only in realizing creative or experiential values, but in attitudinal values as well. The very way in which a man faces his destiny creates, for him, the opportunity of realizing values and hence of finding a meaning in life. One of the major tenets of logotherapy might be expressed in these words: "There are no circumstances whatsoever that limit man's capacity to take a stand toward his condition." This thesis was given ample support in the concentration camp experiences. Noting that in such situations creative and experiential values are practically negated ("There is nothing else to do but to shovel, and nothing else to experience but punishment, hunger, and cold."), Frankl goes on to assert the essential freedom that still remains for man:

In the realization of attitudinal values he is free—free "from" all conditions and circumstances, and free "to" the inner mastery of his destiny, "to" proper upright suffering. This freedom knows no conditions, it is a freedom "under all circumstances" and until the last breath.[9]

Countless heroic souls have demonstrated the superiority of the spirit over the infirmities of the body as they have faced certain death. Frankl tells of a young professional man, dying slowly with an inoperable spinal tumor, leading to progressive paralysis, who had long ago been forced to give up his career and the opportunity for realizing creative values. But during his illness he devoted himself to the realization of experiential values with good music, good books, and stimulating contacts with other patients. When finally the paralysis made even these activities impossible, the last remaining meaning in life was in attitudinal value.

He now set himself the role of adviser to his fellow sufferers, and in every way strove to be an exemplar to them. He bore his own suffering bravely. The day before his death—which he foresaw—he knew that the doctor on duty had been ordered to give him an injection of morphine at night. . . . When the doctor came to see him on his afternoon round, the patient asked him to give him the injection in the evening—so that the doctor would not have to interrupt his night's rest just on his account.[10]

A woman bookkeeper faced death in a similar spirit. In the advanced stages of tuberculosis with certain death looming up before her, she wrote:

When was my life richer? All that time when I was frightfully useful, and had so many duties that I didn't know what to do? Or, in those last years of spiritual struggle with a thousand problems? Even the struggle to conquer the fear of death, which has tormented, hunted and haunted me to an inconceivable degree—even this struggle seems to me to have been more valuable than all my professional achievements.[11]

In a similar way an extraordinarily brilliant young mathematician writes in a letter of his reactions when he discovered accidentally that his situation was medically hopeless:

I get this last chance to test my fighting spirit, only this is a fight where the question of victory is ruled out at the start. Rather, it's a last exertion of a simple strength, a last gymnastic drill as it were. I want to bear the pain without narcotics as long as it is at all possible. "A fight for a lost cause?" In terms of our philosophy, that phrase has to be stricken off the books. The fighting alone is what counts. There cannot be any lost causes. . . . In the evening we played Bruckner's Fourth, the *Romantic Symphony*. I was filled with emotion of love for all mankind, a sense of cosmic vastness. For the rest, I work away at mathematics and don't give way to sentimentality.[12]

Sometimes it takes the direct intervention of a strong personality to mobilize attitudinal values. With the Bethesda invalid, Jesus' encouragement was centered in a direct challenge: "Rise, take up your pallet, and walk," followed later by the injunction: "Sin no more, that nothing worse befall you" (i.e., don't run from life anymore). Anyone who has known in his own life the impact of a strong, loving person who speaks with authority can appreciate the immediate response of the invalid to Jesus. And if personal experience does not supply such evidence, the story of the transformation of a woman like Elizabeth Barrett by young Robert Browning from totally incapacitating illness to vigorous health is testimony enough.[13]

It is not clear just how the Bethesda invalid was healed. Indeed, in a scientific age, the reports of miraculous healing are always difficult for reason to grasp. It may, indeed, be true that the invalid recovered in a miraculous fashion. Many a cure accomplished today by medical science or indeed through spontaneous recovery appears miraculous and often defies explanation.[14] It is not by happenstance that the new developments in pharmacology have gone under the name of "miracle drugs." We have indicated before, however, that the New Testament record is to be understood best not in its literal but in its figurative or symbolic sense. This seems to me to be especially true in dealing with the physical miracles. Whatever else happened, here is a man in need who was helped. In the presence of Jesus of Nazareth, a distressed person was helped in ways that seemed miraculous. The specific details themselves are unimportant. Whether a man is freed from a disabling symptom or from an unhealthy outlook, in either case he is helped. If the help came in the direction of a reactivation of the "defiant power of the human spirit," who is to say that that is less important than the restoration of physical locomotion? And if the help is such that a man's total life is changed in the spiritual dimensions (without sin before God) as well as on the interpersonal level (bearing suffering without complaint) who is to say that his physical health remains untouched?

X. Restoring Man's Dignity

The Gerasene Demoniac; Mark 5:1-20

Although the story of the encounter of Jesus with the Gerasene demoniac is clothed in the thought patterns of a pre-scientific age, the predicament of one who feels himself possessed by a power outside of himself is well known in our own day. The biblical term "demon-possessed" is useful as a graphic description of the sense of helplessness that some know so well. Moreover, the joining of the story of the Gerasene demoniac with folklore about the destruction of a herd of swine is easily understood when we consider the folklore which gathers even today around mental illness.[1]

The task to which Jesus addressed himself with the demoniac was the restoration of the man's sense of human dignity. The rediscovery of the dignity of man is one of the major achievements of our times. It is to the credit of existentialist thinkers like Frankl that, without discounting the contributions made by the psychological approach that studied man as an instinct-directed animal, the real essence of man is to be found in those very characteristics which distinguish him from the animal. An animal, as Frankl says in agreement with Max Scheler, has an environment, but man has a world.[2] It is man with a conscience, man making free decisions, man accepting personal responsibility, who is dealt with in the most adequate kind of psychotherapy. It is man in the biblical image, made only a little lower than the angels, crowned with glory and honor (Ps. 8:5).

It is when man is robbed of his dignity that he becomes ill. One of the clearest evidences of this fact is to be found among older, retired people who, living in a culture that tends to equate personal significance with productive usefulness, feel useless and hence deprived of their dignity. Given even a small amount of recognition so that dignity is returned, it is amazing how the physical organism responds with a new vitality that brings the bedridden to his feet or empties the wheelchair of its premature occupancy. Or consider the delinquent whose sense of dignity has been so offended by an unresponsive society that he seeks recognition in antisocial ways, turning his anger against his fellowmen. Or consider the illness that is neither organic nor social but rather psychic, the illness of psychosis. Here, again, the dignity of a human being has been injured, his sense of personal adequacy has been undermined, his freedom to be unique has been curtailed. Now his anger is not turned outward toward his world but is turned in against himself. Angry at himself, at war with himself, he feels only the conflict of the unresolved forces struggling within his makeup and loses sight of the essential unity that dignity implies. The only name which seems to make sense to him is "Legion; for we are many" (Mark 5:9*b*).

When mental illness is conceived of as a loss of human dig-

nity, then the indicated approach becomes clearer.[3] When angry behavior is recognized as an expression of the fear that human dignity is to be even more impaired, then a method to follow is indicated. I have often watched the transformation in mental patients from what appeared to be angry assaultiveness to eager receptivity when the apparent anger was understood as fear and approached accordingly. When it was demonstrated clearly that the fear was unnecessary, the angry attack was replaced by requests for help. Often the best therapeutic agent was the tiny student nurse who, obviously, could do the patient no harm. But even more often the change took place in the presence of a therapeutically oriented person whose whole manner indicated an acceptance of the patient and reflected an appraisal of dignity and worth for him. So it must have been with the demoniac of the Gerasenes whose wild ravings were completely subdued in the patient and understanding (and hence fearless) approach of Jesus.

The change that can take place in a psychotic person in the presence of a truly therapeutic person is vividly illustrated by Carroll Wise as he tells of watching the psychiatrist Harry Stack Sullivan at work. Sullivan was visiting Worcester State Hospital when a schizophrenic patient was being presented to the staff. The doctor making the presentation was unable to get any communication from the patient. With a shrug of futility he turned to Sullivan with an unspoken offer for the visiting doctor to try his hand. Wise describes what followed:

Sullivan's first move was to edge his chair just a little closer to that of the patient and to lean forward so that he could look directly at the patient in a very friendly, warm manner. To the amazement of all, the patient responded to every question and comment that was made by Dr. Sullivan. For half an hour or more they conversed together, seemingly oblivious to the fact that there was anyone else in the room.[4]

Perhaps the key to Sullivan's success was noted by Wise in his preliminary comment, the edging closer and the leaning forward. By his actions Sullivan was saying: "Here is a person worth talking with." I recall vividly a young girl of eighteen who, as a patient in a mental hospital, was as unhappy as a person can be. Approaching her one day as the hospital chaplain I tried to initiate conversation, but she rejected me with the angry words: "Go away! I don't want to talk with you!" And to make herself very clear, she turned her chair so that it faced the wall. My first impulse was to leave, but then, remembering that she was sick, I turned my chair, too, sat beside her facing the blank wall, and began to talk. Half an hour later when I rose to go she reached for my arm, clutched my coat sleeve and pleaded: "Don't go away. Don't leave me alone." The earlier angry outburst was prompted by her fear that she was unacceptable, that no one would want to talk with her. Here, in a mild form, is the same kind of resistance to potential help that the demoniac demonstrated when he cried out: "What have you to do with me? . . . Do not torment me" (Mark 5:7).

The story of the Gerasene demoniac has the ring of authenticity about it. When Jesus asked: "What is your name?" he was really asking the kind of a question that a modern therapist would ask. Leslie Weatherhead translates the question as follows: " 'What is thy name?' is the equivalent of the question a modern therapist would ask: 'How did it all begin? What

105

power is it that has dominion over you?' " [5] It may very well
be that Jesus, who had sought refuge from the crowds by going
to the wilderness of the Gerasenes, spent most of the night exploring with this pitiful man the story of his life in the pattern
of contemporary psychotherapy. Weatherhead, for example, believes that the demoniac may have been helped to bring forth
long repressed emotions, perhaps related to atrocities committed by Roman legionnaires.[6] Like some servicemen suffering
in our own time from battle trauma, a violent emotional catharsis
sometimes results in a complete cure.

Whether the causal factors of the illness were ever really
uncovered or not, the final scene showing the "demoniac" restored to normalcy, sitting talking with Jesus, suggests the re-
newal of communication, the breakthrough from isolation to
interpersonal relationships. Here, in Jesus, was a man with whom
he could talk freely about his innermost feelings; here was an
acceptance of him even in the depths of his being, depths which
he could not look at alone.

It was important to him that Jesus was not afraid of him. The
people were, both when he was sick and later when he had been
restored to health. In their fear they had banished him outside
of the city; and even when he was well they were uncertain
about him and hesitant to accept him. Fearful of the impulses
that raged unchecked within himself, he could not be helped
by those who also feared him, but only by one who stood outside
of the fear, who could understand it but was not drawn into it.
And this Jesus could do, for he knew the depths of man, the
potential for good and bad, the intensity of loves and hates, the
mixture of tenderness and hostility, the struggle of egotism and
altruism. Sensing the unchecked anger that was driving the

man, Jesus could confront him calmly with a direct approach: "You are angry, but you don't have to be ruled by anger." ("Come out of the man, you unclean spirit.")

It was as if Jesus was saying to him: "You are not accountable for your feelings, they are a part of your sickness which you cannot control. But you are responsible for your attitude toward them." This is the approach which Frankl follows. He believes that even the schizophrenic retains a residue of freedom for confronting his illness.

Even the manifestations of psychosis conceal a real spiritual person, unassailable by mental disease. Only the possibility of communication with the outside world and of self-expression are inhibited by the disease; the nucleus of man remains indestructible. The schizophrenic, as well as the manic-depressive, has a remnant of freedom with which he can confront his illness and realize himself, not only in spite of it but because of it.[7]

Thus Frankl is able to say to a young schizophrenic artist:

Don't focus on questions like what pathological events might be there and of what kind. You are a spiritually struggling, artistically creative mind. Beyond that there is disease. Leave it to us to cure you from it. Don't be concerned with your strange feelings and with the question of what they might mean. Ignore them until we make you rid of them. Devote your thoughts to the great and marvelous things which you are to create.[8]

Indeed, in asserting that the attitude toward life is the area with which to work, even with the psychotic, Frankl is underscoring a point of view which Anton Boisen has been pressing for decades. Boisen sees acute mental disturbances, including his own,[9] as indications of an inner struggle to grasp the meaning of life in a personal way. As such, acute psychotic episodes rather than being merely indicators of unhealthy disturbances in a self-system, may be evidence of a struggle toward a rebirth, an effort at assimilating hitherto unassimilated aspects of the personality into a unified and meaningful whole. It is as if a recognition of irreconcilable trends demands a full stop in normal life patterns until some satisfactory resolution can be worked out.

If life does not make sense, if there seems to be no meaning to personal existence, then emotional illness easily fills the void. Frankl treated a seventeen-year-old Jewish youth, a student of the Talmud, who had been through Nazi persecution followed by two and a half years in a mental hospital. Following discharge he was unable to reestablish himself in any normal pattern of life, blaming God for making him different. Frankl helped him to see his plight in a meaningful light.

Who knows whether it was not quite good for you, for you had to be brought nearer to yourself and finally to find yourself. Weren't you more careless before in your way of life? Whereas now you have become a more earnest and thoughtful personality. Is it inconceivable that through the two and a half years of confinement God wanted to confront you with a task; perhaps your confinement was your assignment for that period of your life. . . . Your study of the Talmud will from now on be easier and yet will penetrate deeper into its wisdom. . . . For now you have been purified like gold and silver. . . . Through your tears which you wept, the clinkers were removed from your old self.[10]

Frankl's rationale for the treatment of this young student was called forth by a comment made by a visiting psychiatrist. The visitor noted that when the boy left the office he was different; he had definitely changed during the interview. The doctor noted further that Frankl had gripped the essential point and had helped the boy to find purpose and to view his plight in terms of purpose. In response Dr. Frankl said:

I heightened his self-esteem, not by pointing to the patient's state of affairs which was sad, but by making gleam the potential meaning which needed to be fulfilled by that boy despite his mental disease and its residues. I didn't so much analyze what the walls were like which separated him from life and the outside world. Neither did I care for the origin of these walls, that is, the psychosis and the psychogenesis, and the psychodynamics; I rather tried to challenge the patient out of his walls, helping him transcend them, and finally meeting the demands of a meaningful life of his own.[11]

Helped in seeing some meaning in his suffering, the young Talmudic student was then able to pick up the threads of his life and resume a pattern that was quite normal in most respects. That is, Frankl had helped the patient to detach himself from the psychotic processes which were affecting him by mobilizing the distinctly human capacity, present even in psychosis, to take a stand against the illness. Citing another patient, a man whose jealousy was of paranoid dimensions so that friends feared he would kill his wife, Frankl notes that when the wife became ill the jealous husband suddenly became devoted to her, caring for her with real tenderness. Frankl then observes:

What one makes out of a psychosis, whether one gives in and yields to that which psychotic delusions and hallucinations whisper in one's ear, as it were, or which steps one takes and in which direction under the influence of a psychosis—all this depends ultimately and solely on the spiritual core of the personality involved.[12]

It comes as no secret that conflicting claims are resolved when reference to the spiritual (noetic) dimension is made. Even in psychosis an orientation to the world of values can exercise a controlling influence over behavior. Frankl reports on a sixty-year-old schizophrenic man who had heard voices for decades, who was regarded as an idiot by all around. It was noted, however, that even though he was often overexcited, he regained control while he was singing in a choir with his sister. When Dr. Frankl asked him for whose sake he controlled himself, expecting to hear that it was because of his dearly beloved sister, the patient answered instead: "For God's sake!" Even in his sickness, he had a sense of the claim of God upon his life.

It was not by chance that Jesus admonished the young man who had been considered a demoniac to consider his life in the light of God's mercy toward him. We have seen continually in the Gospel record how man's problems are never considered as solved except as they are viewed from a more than human perspective. The logotherapeutic approach aims at more than a mere change of behavior patterns, it is a complete reorientation to a life of a broader spectrum. It is introducing the concept of a relationship to a larger world than the world in which scientific man normally lives. It is seeing man in the largest possible perspective.

It is not strange that the man of the Gerasenes wanted to stay with Jesus. Having found someone who had helped him to accept himself and to see himself related in a more meaningful way to life, he wanted to hold on to this new interpreter of life.

But Jesus would have none of it. The real test of life, he knew so well, was in the resumption of daily tasks, at home among old friends. But even here the pattern of life was changed, for now the man was no longer preoccupied with his own troubles but was commissioned to tell of the changes that God had made in his life. His orientation was now no longer on himself but on his relationship with God. No wonder that men marveled at the transformation.

XI. Exercising Man's Freedom
Jesus as Servant; John 13:3-5, 12-16

One of the revolutionary teachings of Jesus was that greatness comes through service. The dramatic act of personal service in washing the disciples' feet was nothing new for Jesus; from the decision laid down at the time of his temptation through the last moments of ministry to a fellow sufferer on a cross, Jesus gave the highest priority to service. In taking a towel and washing his disciples' feet, he was exercising his freedom to choose how to use his life. His choice was clear: he would find fulfillment in serving the needs of his fellow men and, hence, in serving God. In the symbolic act of service he reinforced, by his action, the emphasis which had been a basic element in his teaching. Like any good teacher, he underscored the concept by demonstrating it. He knew how hard it is for most people to accept the way of service as the way of life; he knew that a dramatic act was needed to call the attention of his disciples to the priority which he gave to service. And when the disciples began disputing about "which of them was to be regarded as the greatest" (Luke 22:24b), he knew that he had to clarify their erroneous orientation.

Most neurotic suffering results from an erroneous outlook. In one way or another the neurotic has acquired a picture of his place in life which simply isn't true. Feeling helpless in the midst of conflicting claims, he allows his life to be molded by circumstances until he feels himself to be little more than a victim of fate. Educated in a scientific age he easily falls prey to the error of determinism, whether biological, psychological, or sociological, seeing himself as caught by the limitations of physical defects or crippled by emotional conditioning or imprisoned in cultural patterns. Uncertain of his own powers he drifts into patterns of relationship that are ineffective or even destructive and which become set like ruts frozen in deep mud. Even when he recognizes the inappropriateness of inflexible behavior, his view of life is such that he sees himself as powerless to change.

It is quite clear that Jesus gave primary attention to correcting a wrong view of life. Whether dealing with the rich young ruler, or with the Samaritan woman, or with Martha, or with Simon the Pharisee, or with the demoniac of the Gerasene, or with the disciples, the record is very clear: his major concern was to help them to see life from another perspective. Moreover, in those incidents where no extended conversation is indicated, it is clear that a conversation must have taken place (i.e., with Zacchaeus and the paralyzed youth and the Bethesda invalid). And in each instance Jesus was never satisfied with minor changes but always pointed to the most fundamental sort of reorientation. So he challenged the rich young ruler to cut loose from his dependence on things, and the Samaritan woman to seek meaning on a more primary level than sex, and Zacchaeus to find life by reestablishing the ties of community relationships. Wherever people were moving down dead-end roads, he pointed out their error and helped them to find a new pathway.

Is there any reason to believe that the neurotic of today needs anything less? Can any therapy really serve its purpose if unrealistic views of life are left unchallenged, if inappropriate behavior patterns go unchecked? It is the assertion of logotherapy that a major part of the therapeutic task lies in correcting false views of life, in challenging inadequate philosophies. Recognizing how an individual's vision is limited by his own life experience, Frankl perceives the therapeutic task as including the marshaling of arguments to challenge destructive world views and declares: "We have therefore attempted to counter the basic skepticism so frequently expressed by our patients, and to develop the counter-arguments necessary to blunt the edge of ethical nihilism." [1] In this sense, logotherapy supplements psychotherapy as it is normally conceived, and fits more into the pattern of the habitual ministry of Jesus than do most of the contemporary theories in the therapeutic world. Thus Frankl says:

While the task of psychotherapy is to uncover the psychological background of an ideology, the task of logotherapy is to reveal the flaws in improper logical grounds for a world-view and thereby to effect a readjustment of that view. [2]

Frankl illustrates the typical logotherapeutic approach in the case of a highly intellectual teacher who was being treated for recurrent depressions of an organic origin. The first approach was somatic, prescribing a drug (opium). It became apparent, however, that her reaction to her depression was the basic problem, hence psychotherapy was indicated.

Once psychotherapy was introduced, much that this patient had locked within herself was released. She herself disclosed her whole spiritual distress—her low opinion of herself, the poverty of content and meaning in her life—the dreary existence of a person who felt herself hopelessly handicapped by these recurrent depressions to which fate had condemned her.[3]

Frankl's approach was to instruct the patient to "ignore as far as possible her depressive mood, and above all to avoid unhappy brooding about her depression," but he went far beyond this, entering now the field of logotherapy.

What was now indicated was a procedure that went beyond psychotherapeutic treatment in the narrower sense of the word. Here was a case where logotherapeutic treatment was necessary. It was the doctor's business to show the patient that her very affliction —these fated recurrent depressions—posed a challenge for her. Since men are free to take a rational position on psychic processes, she was free to take a positive attitude toward it. Her destiny should direct her to the conscious and responsible shaping of her life in spite of inner difficulties that shadowed it.[4]

Frankl concludes the case report with these words:

After this existential analysis—for that was what it was—she was able, in spite of and even during further phases of endogenous depression, to lead a life that was more conscious of responsibility and more filled with meaning than before treatment. . . . One day this patient was able to write to her doctor: "I was not a human being until you made me one." [5]

This final testimony of the teacher reminds us of the phrase in the New Testament Parable of the Prodigal Son: "He came to himself . . ." (Luke 15:17). Indeed, Frankl asserts that whereas psychoanalysis aims at helping man to " 'come to terms with' his id . . . existential analysis aims primarily at man's 'coming to himself'—at his arriving first of all at an understanding of his own ego," [6] that is, of understanding and utilizing the most distinctly human aspect of the self. When the prodigal son "came to himself," he recognized error in his life orientation and set out to correct it in a responsible way.

It is clear that such a change involves one's whole outlook on life, and that such a change can be effected only by a counseling procedure that looks on life in its fullest dimensions. A basic criticism of much that goes on in the current therapeutic world is that its outlook on life is narrowly defined in rather rigid ways. So a Freudian approach would reduce all life to the narrow confines of a biological drive; and a Jungian approach would see life in terms of the expression of drives originating in the collective unconscious; and an Adlerian approach would interpret life in terms of the power drive; and a Sullivanian approach would see life in terms of security operations. To be sure, each of these approaches has significant insights to contribute to the understanding of the complex human personality, but each one errs in insisting on seeing all of life through its individual lense. The fact is that life needs to be looked at on more than one dimension; it is for this reason that Frankl has developed a dimensional ontology, a way of looking at human existence that preserves the unity of the self yet permits analysis from more than one perspective.[7]

Dimensional ontology is based on the principle of understanding reality by employing several different perspectives. If a ball, a cylinder, and a cone, for example, are viewed from the side, they appear as three distinct objects, each one radically different in shape from the other. But these three objects, when viewed from directly above, all assume the same round shape. If the only perspective employed is from above, then no distinction in shape is visible and the assumption is that the three are alike. When, however, the side perspective is added, it immediately becomes apparent that three quite different objects are involved.

In an analogous way, the human person may be viewed from a perspective which minimizes, even obliterates any differences in being; on the other hand, the human person may be viewed from a perspective in which it becomes readily apparent that three different aspects are to be distinguished. To be more specific, the human being can be conceived of only as a biological organism, an animal like any other animal. Malfunctioning of the organism is to be treated solely by somatic means, by drugs, or by electric current (shock), or by surgery. All ills are treated as being somatogenic (originating in the body). Or, in the second place, the human being may be approached primarily as a psychic mechanism, a being whose emotional nature is disturbed, whose behavior pattern is judged in terms of unconscious repressions or of compensatory mechanisms. All illness is interpreted in psychological terms, and all treatment is based on the uncovering of psychological trauma. Or, in the third place, the human being may be seen solely as a spiritual (noetic) being, whose condition in life is dictated entirely by his relationship to the world of meaning. Every illness is then conceived of as a violation of man's system of values or as a total absence of meaningful relationships to life.[8]

It is clear that each of these perspectives has its share of truth. The problem comes, however, when any one of the approaches is used to the exclusion of the others. The fact is that the human person cannot be captured without drawing in all three levels. Man is not solely body or mind or spirit but, on the contrary, is all three at the same moment. As the incident of the paralyzed youth shows so clearly, physical disability may easily reflect an unresolved emotional entanglement and an unanswered question about life. As is shown in the treatment procedure used with the teacher cited above, all three dimensions must often be entered to effect a cure; and this is precisely Frankl's method.

There is another sense in which his dimensional concept corrects inadequate views of life. Whereas some therapeutic procedures center on man himself and the struggle going on within his own psyche, others would stress the problems in relating to significant persons in the environment, and still others would stress the broader relationships with the world at large. A major part of the effectiveness of the ministry of Jesus is that he never lost sight of all three areas. His approach was always very personal, yet before he was through he had drawn attention away from self-preoccupation to the broader dimensions of interpersonal living, all perceived within a framework that explored the primary relationship with God.

Indeed, it was the stress on the relationship with God which gave a uniqueness to his message. Over and over again he interjected the claims of God on a person's life into his conversations. It was not only in his personal temptations that he brought God into the picture, but in every circumstance in life. It is as if he were saying: "Of course you can read life without God, but it isn't an adequate reading!" Indeed, if there is any meaning at all in life, it stems from God. It is because logotherapy does permit this affirmation that we have made more use of it than of any school of psychotherapy.

Frankl has asserted from time to time that logotherapy is not a religious therapy but that it is, rather, a therapy that opens the door to religion. We have already noted that when Frankl uses the word "spiritual" it is to be conceived in the noetic sense rather than with any strictly religious meaning. Frankl notes, however, that the religious person is one who has simply gone farther in his affirmations than his non-religious comrade. He uses the illustration of the mountain climber who is willing to proceed to the very highest peak although it might be hidden by fog. He does so with a resounding "aye" on his lips; he says "yes" to God.[9]

The ultimate meaning in life is to be found, as Jesus asserts and as logotherapy underscores, in the more-than-human world. The very fact that some values are more significant than others points to a hierarchy of values and assumes that one value is supreme, namely, God. John's Gospel makes Jesus' position very clear: "Knowing that . . . he had come from God and was going to God [he] . . . girded himself with a towel." Frankl uses the illustration of the point of perspective that lies outside a picture but gives proportion to the picture. In like manner, God stands outside of human life but gives meaning to all of life.[10] Any view of life that makes any value other than God absolute creates the fallacy of absolutizing what is really only relative. According to Frankl, this is the main source of any despair. For example, the unmarried woman who despairs over her single state has made a relative value (marriage) into an absolute one, has confused something secondary with something primary.

Indeed, there are some who would so read life in terms of man that even God, himself, is depicted in terms of man's experience. Thus some would say that man's image of God is totally conditioned by the circumstances of his life. Thus if the relationship with an earthly father has been negative, the relationship with the heavenly Father will also be negative. But the facts contradict this theory. Frankl cites a brief study which demonstrates conclusively that even the worst father image need not stand in the way of the development of a positive relationship with God, and that the best relationship with a father does not necessarily lead to a good relationship with God. In the study, one half of the people studied did not develop a religious life in accord with their father image. Five times as many resisted the influence of their father image in relating to God as followed it.[11] Rather than saying that the God-image results from the father-image, the truth of the matter is more likely to be found in the reverse: that "the father relationship is an inadequate representation of the God-image relationship."[12] In biblical terms: "We love, because he first loved us" (I John 4:19).

It is this tendency to see all of life through the eyes of man rather than through the eyes of God that Jesus objected to so strongly. And it is the same tendency in life today that leads Frankl to assert that often the "basis of neurotic existence is in a deficiency of the patient's relationship to transcendence."[13] Frankl sees a need for delving into the unconscious, but adds the dimension of the spiritual unconscious to the more commonly accepted psychological realm.

Basic as the relationship to God was, Jesus nevertheless began his contacts with people on a direct, more personal plane. The washing of his disciples' feet was more than just a symbolic act. The personalized approach is the most characteristic trait in the ministry of Jesus. Over and over again, in the midst of a crowd, he singled out individuals and related to them. His awareness of the one woman who touched him even while the crowd was pressing in on him (Mark 5:25-34) is typical of his sensitivity to individuals. In the midst of the Jericho crowd, it was Jesus who singled out Zacchaeus and called him by name. Among the throng at the Pool of Bethesda, a single sufferer was ministered to. In the crowded courtyard of the high priest it was only Peter who was called to account and at the same time ministered to by the look of love.

In an even more significant sense, the ministry of Jesus was never stereotyped; he seldom ministered to individuals in the same way. He followed no pattern but responded to individual need in whatever seemed the natural and appropriate way. He counted on no technique but rather on a personal relationship. His approach was the very opposite of any studied objectivity; he gave himself fully to each relationship, improvising from the circumstances in which he found himself and with what resources he had available. It is easy to imagine that his choicest parables were prompted by current scenes: a farmer sowing, a house built on a rock cliff, a Pharisee praying; and that his teaching was in response to specific situations of need.

The importance of the individual, of course, was the cornerstone of his teachings. When logotherapy stresses the personal will to meaning it is only reaffirming the Christian assertion of the irreplaceability of each individual person. Not only is there a life task lying in wait for every person, but that particular life task remains unfulfilled wherever it is not put into practice. Man is called into a responsible fulfillment of his particular task in life.

Indeed, it is the need for a personalized approach to life that instigated the existentialist movement in philosophy. Disillusioned by scientific objectivity that reduced man to a cog in a machine, a mere cell in the organism, and dissatisfied with the speculative philosophy that lost sight of the individual in its consideration of the cosmos,[14] existentialism has insisted on viewing life through the eyes of individual man, unprejudiced by preconceived notions. Man, in the existentialist view, is seen as free, free from the control of the past and free to work out his own future.

We have noted again and again the directness with which Jesus put the challenge. In the account in John's Gospel (John 21:15-22) of a final meeting of Peter with Jesus, following the resurrection, Peter is reported to have held back with delaying questions, but Jesus said simply, "What is that to you? Follow me." And to follow meant to "feed my sheep," to get going in the life of service. In a similar way the basis of logotherapeutic treatment lies in a focus on worthwhile goals that precludes preoccupation with symptoms. Meaning in life can never be found through purely speculative thought. It is discovered in the act of commitment. "Go! Sell! Give! Come! Follow!" and the meaning in life is found!

In Frankl's own life there is validation for the power of the act of commitment. He tells of how the loss of his first major manuscript in the concentration camp led to living out his thoughts rather than writing them.

It did not even seem possible, let alone probable, that the manuscript of my first book which I had hidden in my coat when I arrived at Auschwitz would ever be rescued. Thus, I had to undergo and to overcome the loss of my spiritual child. And now it seemed as if nothing and no one would survive me; neither a physical nor a spiritual child of my own! So I found myself confronted with the question whether under such circumstances my life was ultimately void of any meaning.

Not yet did I notice that an answer to this question with which I was wrestling so passionately was already in store for me, and that soon thereafter this answer should be given to me. This was the case when I had to surrender my clothes and in turn inherited the wornout rags of an inmate who had been sent to the gas chamber immediately after his arrival at the Auschwitz railway station. Instead of the many pages of my manuscript, I found in a pocket of the newly acquired coat a single page torn out of a Hebrew prayer book, which contained the main Jewish prayer, *Shema Yisrael*. How should I have interpreted such a "coincidence" other than as a challenge to *live* my thoughts instead of merely putting them on paper? [15]

It is quite apparent that Frankl does live his concepts.[16] He has his very human feelings, as every gifted person does, but his capacity to mobilize man's defiant spirit in the face of almost insurmountable odds has been demonstrated over and over again. He stands in the tradition of those who have found meaning in exercising their own freedom.

The Christian faith has always been more than a system of belief. It is a way of life, a responsible and committed way of action. It is life lived under God, life derived from God, life reaching out toward God. The real secret of the personal ministry of Jesus can never be understood apart from his closeness to God. He found freedom for his life, as he first of all accepted personal responsibility in the search for meaning. And he found meaning as he exercised his freedom, under God, in service.

NOTES

CHAPTER I

1. "The religious man experiences his existence not only as a concrete task but as a personal mission which is given to him by a personal Being. Thus he sees his task transparently, namely, in the light of Transcendence; he alone can in spite of all say 'yes' to life under all conditions and circumstances—in spite of all; in spite of distress and death." Viktor E. Frankl, "The Will to Meaning," *Journal of Pastoral Care*, XII (Summer, 1958), p. 87.
2. *Der Unbewusste Gott*, translated as *The Unconscious God* (Wien: Amandus-Verlag, 1949), p. 74.
3. Viktor E. Frankl, *The Doctor and the Soul* (New York: Alfred A. Knopf, 1957), p. 113.
4. "Group Therapeutic Experiences in a Concentration Camp," *Group Psychotherapy*, VII (May, 1954), 83.
5. *The Doctor and the Soul*, p. 113.
6. "Dachau," *Ladies' Home Journal*, September, 1945.
7. Viktor E. Frankl, *Man's Search for Meaning* (New York: Washington Square Press, 1963), p. 110. This book lists Frankl's writings, pp. 215-20.. Used by permission of Beacon Press.
8. "Group Therapeutic Experiences in a Concentration Camp," p. 88.
9. Cf. Joshua Liebman, *Peace of Mind* (New York: Simon and Schuster, 1946), Chapter III, "Love Thyself Properly."
10. Cf. Frankl, "Beyond Self-Actualization and Self-Expression," *Journal of Existential Psychiatry*, I (Spring, 1960), 5-20.
11. This is the term used by Harry Stack Sullivan, *Conceptions of Modern Psychiatry* (New York: W. W. Norton & Company, 1953), p. 22.

12. *Journals of Kierkegaard* (Torchbook ed. New York: Harper & Row, 1959), p. 23.
13. Cf. Gordon W. Allport, *Becoming* (New Haven: Yale University Press, 1955), p. 47, for an elaboration of the concept of "propriate striving."
14. Ludwig Binswanger, *Sigmund Freud: Reminiscences of a Friendship* (New York: Grune and Stratton, 1957), p. 81.
15. *Der Unbewusste Gott*, p. 88. See also *The Doctor and the Soul*, p. xvii: "I myself feel that humanity has demonstrated *ad nauseam* in recent years that it has instincts, drives. Today it appears more important to remind man that he has a spirit, that he is a spiritual being."

CHAPTER II

1. *The Great Enterprise* (New York: W. W. Norton & Company, 1952), p. 72.
2. Edwin Markham, "Outwitted," *The Shoes of Happiness* (New York: Doubleday, Doran, 1928), p. 1. Reprinted by permission of Virgil Markham.
3. Harry Stack Sullivan *The Psychiatric Interview* (New York: W. W. Norton & Company, 1954), p. 102.
4. Quoted by Frankl in *Homo Patiens* tr. Donald Tweedie, (Wien: Franz Deuticke, 1950), p. 17.
5. John Steinbeck, *East of Eden* (Chicago: Sears Readers Club, 1952), p. 303.
6. Frankl, "Existence and Values: Foundations of Logotherapy," manuscript in preparation, p. 29.
7. *Ibid.*, p. 105.
8. Martin Buber, as quoted by Maurice S. Friedman, *Martin Buber: The Life of Dialogue* (Torchbook ed. New York: Harper & Row, 1960), p. 191.
9. In Stanley W. Standal and Raymond Corsini, eds., *Critical Incidents in Psychotherapy* (Englewood Cliffs, N.J.: Prentice-Hall, 1959), pp. 3, 6. Note also this entire book.
10. Frankl likes to use this descriptive word.
11. Cf. Carroll E. Wise, *Psychiatry and the Bible* (New York: Harper & Row, 1956), p. 91, who makes a similar distinction between the acceptance of the corner tavern as contrasted with the acceptance of Christian Fellowship.
12. In *The Doctor and the Soul*, p. 105.
13. Cf. Matt. 5:23-24.

CHAPTER III

1. Carl G. Jung, *Modern Man in Search of a Soul* (New York: Harcourt, Brace, 1939), p. 70.
2. *Letters of Sigmund Freud*, Ernest L. Freud, ed. (New York: Basic Books, 1960), p. 436.
3. "Existential Dynamics and Neurotic Escapism," (mimeographed) address delivered in New York at the Academy of Religion and Mental Health, May 17, 1962; published in the *Journal of Existential Psychiatry*, IV (Summer, 1963), 28.
4. Cf. Frankl's reference to the "spiritual dimension" in his exposition of "dimensional ontology," "On Logotherapy and Existential Analysis," *American Journal of Psychoanalysis*, XVIII (1958), 28-29.
5. The German word is *geistig* (spiritual, non-ecclesiastical) as contrasted with *geistlich* (spiritual, ecclesiastical).
6. *Man's Search for Meaning*, p. 164.
7. *Existential Psychology*, Rollo May, ed. (New York: Random House, 1961), p. 95.
8. *Loc. cit.*; cf. also Carl G. Jung, *The Undiscovered Self* (Boston: Little, Brown, 1958).
9. Reuel Howe, *Man's Need and God's Action* (Greenwich, Conn.: Seabury, 1953), p. 24.
10. Harry Stack Sullivan, *Conceptions of Modern Psychiatry*, p. 54.
11. Note, however, that the ministry of Jesus is based on the kind of respect for the individual which is at the heart of the "non-directive" approach of Carl Rogers. Cf. Carl Rogers, *Client-Centered Therapy* (Boston: Houghton-Mifflin, 1951).
12. *The Doctor and the Soul*, p. x.
13. "Logotherapy and the Challenge of Suffering," *Review of Existential Psychology and Psychiatry*, I (Winter, 1961), 6.
14. Cf. Frankl, *The Doctor and the Soul*: "It is life that asks questions of man. The individual is not required to question; rather he is questioned by life and has to respond—to be responsible to life." P. 70. "We have here an essential characteristic of the religious man who is conscious of and responsible toward the taskmaster as well as toward his life mission." P. 67.
15. Cf. Harry Overstreet, *The Great Enterprise*, p. 179, who writes that the task was one of "getting rid of the trappings of power and privilege that separated him from his human kind and throwing in his lot with those who dared to affirm love and brotherhood as the central realities of existence."

CHAPTER IV

1. *Man's Search for Meaning*, p. 117.
2. Quoted, *ibid.*, p. 121.
3. "On Logotherapy and Existential Analysis," p. 33.
4. "Existential Dynamics and Neurotic Escapism," p. 30.
5. *The Doctor and the Soul*, p. xix. Frankl also quotes Robert J. Lifton who comments on experiences of American prisoners in North Korea prisoner-of-war camps: "There were examples among them both of altruistic behavior as well as the most primitive forms of struggle for survival." *Ibid.*
6. Edith Weisskopf-Joelson (Purdue University), "Psychology and the Insights of Religion," unpublished mimeographed lecture, November 13, 1959, p. 1. Cf. also Erik Erikson, *Childhood and Society* (New York: W. W. Norton & Company, 1950): "The patient of today suffers most under the problem of what he should believe in and who he should—or, indeed, might—be or become; while the patient of early psychoanalysis suffered most under inhibitions which prevented him from being what and who he thought he knew he was." P. 239.
7. Frankl notes that his main objection to Freud is not that Freud overlooked the spiritual dimension of man, but that he treated the spiritual as only an epiphenomenon, as a derivative from the instinctual rather than as a primary phenomenon itself. Cf. "Existence and Values: Foundations of Logotherapy," p. 15.
8. In Frankl, *Der Unbewusste Gott*, p. 121, my translation.
9. Unpublished lecture, January 30, 1961. Cf. Henry David Thoreau: "I know of no more encouraging fact than the unquestionable ability of man to elevate his life by a conscious endeavor," quoted by Mary Ellen Chase, *The Lovely Ambition* (New York: W. W. Norton & Company, 1960), p. 64.
10. Man "finds himself only to the extent to which he loses himself in the first place, be it for the sake of something or somebody, for the sake of a cause or a fellowman, or 'for God's sake.'" Frankl, "Psychiatry and Man's Quest for Meaning," *Journal of Religion and Health*, I (January, 1962), 100. See also Frankl's critique of self-actualization and the pleasure principle as goals: "Beyond Self-Actualization and Self-Expression," *Journal of Existential Psychiatry*, I (1960), 5-20.
11. Cf. Donald MacKinnon, "Creativity Research," mimeographed address, June 2, 1959, p. 11.
12. Nathan Ackerman uses this term. He goes on to say: "We have no choice but to reject that part of his (the patient's) sick behavior which is perverted and inhuman" (Standal and Corsini, *op. cit.*, pp. 237-38).

CHAPTER V

1. William Barclay reports in his *The Gospel of Mark* (Edinburgh: Saint Andrew Press, 1962): "The Rabbis had a saying: 'There is no sick man healed of his sickness until all his sins have been forgiven him.'" P. 40.
2. *Psychiatry and the Bible*, p. 66.
3. Cf. Joseph F. Fletcher, "Psychiatry and Religion: Conflict or Synthesis," *Journal of Pastoral Care*, VI (Summer, 1952), 12-18.
4. Reported in Standal and Corsini, *op. cit.*, p. 30. See also Frankl's comment on this incident: "Only after the therapist became active and even emotional did it become clear to the patient that she had acted not only contrary to the customs and rules of society, but also against her own true wishes." *Ibid.*, p. 33.
5. The Reverend Bernard Martin of Geneva in Berlin, March 10, 1961.
6. Cf. Leslie D. Weatherhead, *It Happened in Palestine* (Nashville: Abingdon Press, 1936), p. 93.
7. From an interview recorded in lecture-demonstration, Vienna, Spring, 1961. Cf. Frankl, *The Doctor and the Soul:* "Challenging the meaning of life can . . . never be taken as a manifestation of morbidity or abnormality; it is rather the truest expression of the state of being human." P. 30.
8. Frankl often quoted these familiar words of Augustine.
9. Karen Horney, *Neurosis and Human Growth* (New York: W. W. Norton & Company, 1950), p. 18.
10. Karen Horney, *Our Inner Conflicts* (New York: W. W. Norton & Company, 1945), p. 240.
11. Cf. Earl Loomis, *The Self in Pilgrimage* (New York: Harper & Row, 1960), p. 43. Loomis notes that in the Parable of the Sons and the Father with a Vineyard, the son who flaunts the father at first but then is ready to carry out his wish is acting in the pattern of the healthy adolescent.
12. From the interview cited above, p. 58. See note 7.
13. *Ibid.*

CHAPTER VI

1. Cf. the MacKinnon study cited above, p. 128 note 11.
2. Cf. Frankl, "The Spiritual Dimension in Existential Analysis and Logotherapy," *Journal of Individual Psychology*, XV (November, 1959), 157-65.
3. *The Doctor and the Soul*, p. 160.
4. Cf. Frankl, *Der Unbewusste Gott*, pp. 46-47.
5. Frankl, "The Pleasure Principle and Sexual Neurosis," *International Journal of Sexology*, V (February, 1952), 1-2.
6. "Existence and Values: Foundations of Logotherapy," p. 16.
7. Cf. Frankl's statement: "The two-fold mistake of psychoanalysis is that

it results in an objectification of something which is intrinsically subjective (the person); whereas at the same time an exclusively psychogenetic interpretation of meaning and values must result in the subjectification of something which is intrinsically objective." "Existence and Values: Foundations of Logotherapy," p. 11.

8. Frankl quotes an architect, "Collective Neuroses of the Present Day," *International Journal of Prophylactic Medicine and Social Hygiene,* II (June, 1958), 1.

9. This triad of concepts is Frankl's. He goes on to say: "At the moment when we brought in the 'I ought,' we complemented the subjective aspect of human existence, i.e. being, by its objective counterpart which is meaning." ("Logotherapy and the Challenge of Suffering," p. 3).

10. *The Individual and His Religion: A Psychological Interpretation* (New York: The Macmillan Company, 1950), p. 53.

11. This device, called in logotherapy, "paradoxical intention," is dealt with on pp. 95-96.

12. "On Logotherapy and Existential Analysis," p. 32.

CHAPTER VII

1. From a recorded interview, Summer, 1960. In a slightly different form this case appears in the book *Modern Psychotherapeutic Practice,* Arthur Burton, editor (Palo Alto, California: Science and Behavior Books, 1965).

2. *Man's Search for Meaning,* p. 122.

3. See Chapter VIII for experiential values, and Chapter IX for attitudinal values.

4. Cf. *The Doctor and the Soul,* pp. 106-7, reported in the third person.

5. Cited by Frankl in lecture, November, 1960.

6. Quoted by Frankl, "Collective Neuroses of the Present Day," p. 3.

7. *Ibid.*

8. Cited by Frankl in lecture, November, 1960.

9. Jerome K. Jerome, "The Passing of 'Third Floor Back,' " in *The Saturday Evening Post Treasury* (New York: Simon and Schuster, 1954), pp. 60-68.

10. Frankl, in lecture, March 12, 1961: "By repentance, a man who failed by a deed and cannot remove its outcome, detaches himself from his deed and thereby, from himself. He cannot change what has happened, but he can change himself. He may grow morally."

11. Hugh Missildine, M.D., in unpublished lecture, Columbus, Ohio, March, 1960.

12. *The Meaning of Persons* (New York: Harper & Row, 1957), p. 136.

13. "On Logotherapy and Existential Analysis," p. 29.

14. *Op. cit.,* p. 222.

15. *Ibid.,* pp. 165-66.

CHAPTER VIII

1. *The New Being* (New York: Charles Scribner's Sons, 1955), p. 152.
2. *Psychiatry and the Bible*, p. 49.
3. Betty Friedan, *The Feminine Mystique* (New York: W. W. Norton & Company, 1963), p. 68.
4. Quoted in *ibid.*, p. 28.
5. Frankl, *The Doctor and the Soul*, p. 51.
6. From case demonstration recorded February 14, 1961.
7. "Will to Meaning," p. 86.
8. *Man's Search for Meaning*, p. 93.
9. I Cor. 12:31b–13:1.
10. *The New Being*, p. 153.

CHAPTER IX

1. Quoted by the novelist, Lloyd C. Douglas, who chose from these words the title of his book *Disputed Passage* (Boston: Houghton-Mifflin, 1939).
2. From "Rabbi Ben Ezra," *Complete Poetic and Dramatic Works of Robert Browning* (Boston: Houghton-Mifflin, 1895), p. 384.
3. *The Doctor and the Soul*, p. 2.
4. Cf. Carl G. Jung: "The task of psychotherapy is to connect the conscious attitudes and not to go chasing after infantile memories." *The Practice of Psychotherapy* (New York: Pantheon, 1954), XVI (Bollingen Series), p. 31.
5. Notes of a case presented in class in Vienna in November 30, 1960. Cf. Frankl, "Paradoxical Intention: A Logotherapeutic Technique," *American Journal of Psychotherapy*, XIV (1960), 520-35. See also Robert C. Leslie, "Viktor E. Frankl's New Concept of Man," *motive* (March, 1962), pp. 17-19.
6. Quoted in *The Doctor and the Soul*, p. 129.
7. In conversation, Fall, 1960.
8. Cf. Leslie Weatherhead, *Psychology, Religion and Healing* (Nashville: Abingdon Press, 1951), p. 47.
9. *Homo Patiens*, p. 66.
10. *The Doctor and the Soul*, p. 52. The doctor giving the injection was Frankl himself.
11. *Homo Patiens*, p. 66.
12. *The Doctor and the Soul*, p. 132.
13. Cf. Flanders Dunbar, *Mind and Body: Psychosomatic Medicine* (New York: Random House, 1947), p. 31.
14. Cf. Frankl's report of a patient five years semi-comatose who made a full recovery, *The Doctor and the Soul*, pp. 53-54.

CHAPTER X

1. Although the healing of the demoniac and the destruction of the swine may have taken place at the same time, the causal connection is to be understood not in terms of anything that Jesus did but as a result of the commotion that frightened the swine.

2. Cf. Frankl's "Ten Theses About the Person," *Logos Und Existenz* (Wien: Amandus-Verlag, 1951), Chapter II. For a summary in English of these ten theses, see Donald Tweedie, *Logotherapy and the Christian Faith* (Grand Rapids, Michigan: Baker Book House, 1961), pp. 69-71.

3. Cf. Ernest E. Bruder who notes how Jesus in this incident with the Gerasene demoniac was the one "who . . . paid him the dignity of treating him like a person." "Learning from Deeply Troubled People," *Pastoral Psychology*, XI (November, 1960), pp. 34-35.

4. Carroll A. Wise reviewing Sullivan's *Psychiatric Interview* in *Pastoral Psychology*, V (November, 1954), 57.

5. Weatherhead, *Psychology, Religion and Healing*, p. 55.

6. Weatherhead, *It Happened in Palestine*, p. 117.

7. "Existence and Values: Foundations of Logotherapy," p. 98.

8. From case demonstration recorded, Summer, 1960. See note 1, Chapter VII.

9. See Anton J. Boisen, *Out of the Depths* (New York: Harper & Row, 1960).

10. Recorded notes from Summer, 1960. Frankl compared the patient's hospitalization with the story of Jonah's stay in the whale.

11. Recorded interview of discussion, Summer, 1960.

12. Class lecture, April 4, 1961.

CHAPTER XI

1. *The Doctor and the Soul*, p. 48.

2. *Ibid.*, p. 20 (note).

3. *Ibid.*, pp. 103-4.

4. *Ibid.*

5. *Ibid.*

6. *Ibid.*, p. 100 (note).

7. In "Existential Analysis and Logotherapy," Frankl writes: "In spite of all the ontological variations of the somatic, psychic, and noetic, the anthropological unity and wholeness of a human being are preserved and saved as soon as we make the turn from an analysis of existence to what I call a dimensional ontology." P. 2.

8. Note Frankl's sharp criticism of any approach that sees only spiritual factors in illness. He ridicules the statement by Caruso: "Neurosis is always

(!) an exaggeration of relative values," and that by Daim: "The problem of God is the central problem of conflict in every (!) analysis." "The Will to Meaning," *The Journal of Pastoral Care*, XII (Summer, 1958), 85. The exclamation points are Frankl's.

9. It is to be noted that for Frankl, the Jew, it is man who takes the initiative to move toward God. The Christian insists that God, taking the initiative in Christ, plays a more active role in man's redemption.

10. Cf. *Homo Patiens*, p. 86.

11. This was a study of thirty-six unselected patients studied in a twenty-four-hour period at the Poliklinik in Vienna, November, 1960. The study is reported on in "Existential Dynamics and Neurotic Escapism."

12. Frankl then concludes: "Psychologically speaking the father-child relationship has precedence, but ontologically the relationship reflects and portrays the God-man relationship," *Der Unbewusste Gott*, unpublished translation by Sadler, p. 44.

13. *Ibid.*, p. 103.

14. Cf. Rudolf Allers, *Existentialism and Psychiatry* (Springfield, Illinois: Charles C. Thomas), 1961, p. 18. For a discussion of the personalized approach of Jesus, see Raymond Calkins, *How Jesus Dealt with Men* (Nashville: Abingdon-Cokesbury, 1942).

15. *Man's Search for Meaning*, pp. 181-83.

16. Cf. Jon Carey's book review, " 'Man's Search for Meaning' Is Roadmap for the Future," *San Quentin News*, November 5, 1964: "Professor Frankl writes like a man who lives like he writes."

INDEX

acceptance, 20, 34, 82, 90
Ackerman, Nathan, 128 n. 12
Adler, Alfred, 19, 116
adolescent, 57
alienation, 24
Allers, Rudolf, 133 n. 14
Allport, Gordon
    functional autonomy, 21
    goals, 40
    propriate striving, 21 n. 13
    religious maturity, 69-72
attitudinal values, 76, 92, 97-101
Augustine, 59
Auschwitz, 77, 123

Barclay, William, 128 n. 1
beatnik, 52
Berlin airlift, 36
Berze, Joseph, 77

Bethesda invalid, 92-101, 113, 121
Binswanger, Ludwig, 22
Boisen, Anton, 107-8
Bonaparte, Princess, 39
Browning, Elizabeth Barrett, 100
Browning, Robert, 93, 100
Bruder, Ernest, 132 n. 3
Buber, Martin, 33
Buchenwald, 32

Cain and Abel, 26, 31
Calkins, Raymond, 122 n. 14
cases cited (see also Frankl)
    angry girl in mental hospital,
      105
    father in marital discord, 56
    inmate in state prison, 26-27
    man fearing crossing street, 97

cases cited—*cont'd*
  mental patient plays the fool, 25
  mother with child's life in danger, 66
  prison social worker, 33
  professional woman in Berlin, 36-37
  promiscuous woman, 56
  psychiatrist with therapy group, 42
  serviceman with self-inflicted injury, 56
  student daring to fail, 80
  therapist becoming involved, 82
  woman with guilt over hatred, 56-57
  young matron, 42
  young housewife, 43
cause, devotion to, 74
challenge, 43, 75, 78, 82-83, 109, 114, 122
change, 30, 74, 94
client-centered therapy, 88, 127 n. 11
commitment, 56, 62, 63, 64-73, 122, 124
community, 24, 27-28, 32, 35
communication, 25
concentration camp, 17-18, 32, 44, 47, 48, 76, 82, 98
conscience, 15, 103
Corsini, Raymond, 82, 126 n. 9, 128 n. 12, 129 n. 4

counseling, conditions for, 38
creative values, 74, 76-83, 90, 91, 98
creativity study, 52, 65
critical incident, 34
Cushing, Harvey, 77

Dachau, 17
David, 68, 69
decisions, 13, 21, 23
defensiveness, 53
defiant power of the human spirit, 24, 31-35, 100-101, 109
delinquent, 26, 103
dimensional ontology, 116-17, 127 n. 4
demoniac, see Gerasene
demon-possessed, 102
depth psychology, 14, 27-30, 116
dereflection, 67-68
determinism, 113
dignity restored, 102-4
disciples, 45, 113
Dunbar, Flanders, 131 n. 13

encounter, personal, 81
Erikson, Erik
  ego-identity, 14
  today's patients, 128 n. 6
ego psychology, 52
experiential values, 84, 87-91
existential analysis, 115, 116
existential vacuum, 47, 49-50
existentialism, 102, 122

failure, 75, 79-80

fear, 106
fellowship of acceptance, 45-46, 61
feminine traits, 41, 42
feminine mystique, 86
Fletcher, Joseph, 129 n. 3
forgiveness, 57, 73, 90
Frankl, Viktor; cases cited:
architect strengthens arch, 68-69
concentration camp comrades, 44
despairing nurse, 70-71
dying professional man, 98-99
general practitioner, 48
frigid woman, 67
jealous husband, 109
man overcome by weariness, 88-89
man with sexual neurosis, 67
ornamental painter, 87
rebellious mother, 44-45
resistance fighter, 30
schizophrenic singer, 110
seventeen-year-old girl, 57-59
suicidal painter, 77
Talmud student, 108-9
teacher "made human," 114-15
woman bookkeeper, 99
woman fearing bacteria, 95-96
woman with spiritual interests, 50
young artist, 75, 107
young mathematician, 99

Frankl, Viktor,
bibliography, 125 n. 7
concentration camps, 17
giving injections, 99
God
father-image study, 120
as supreme value, 119
involved as therapist, 81-82
loss of manuscript, 123
optimism about treatment, 96
religious interests, 119
rewriting of manuscript, 76-77
stays to aid patients, 89
freedom
exercising, 112, 122-24
toward conditions, 51, 98
ultimate, 17
Freud, Sigmund
biological drives, 116
categories of illness, 49
determinism, 14
introjection, 14
pleasure principle, 16
questioning meaning, 39
spiritual as epiphenomenon, 128 n. 7
spirituality, 22
Friedan, Betty, 86
Fromm, Erich, 19

geistig, 127 n. 5
Gerasene demoniac, 102-11, 113
Gestapo, 30
Goethe, Johann Wolfgang von, 34, 48, 96

goal, 75
God
  father-image, 120
  forgiveness of, 57, 59
  man-to-man and man-to-God,
    35
  relationship with, 54, 118
  supra meaning, 62
  supreme value, 119
  tasks of, 45
  will of, 19
God-centered orientation, 15, 16,
  39, 41, 111, 124
Group therapy, 70, 88
guilt, 55

Hammerstein, Oscar, 42
health, 92-101
height psychology, 13, 22-23, 60
Hitler, Adolf, 30
Horney, Karen, 19, 60-61
Howe, Reuel, 42
humor, 70

illness, secondary gains, 97
imperative, 43
Iona, 90

Jerome, Jerome K., 130 n. 9
Jesus
  acceptance, 34, 43, 82-83
  candor, 81
  challenge, 43, 61, 78, 82, 100,
    113-14
  confrontation, 51, 54, 107

Jesus—cont'd
  Garden of Gethsemane, 19
  goals, long term, 19
  imperatives, 43
  need for response, 88
  offers personal support, 45
  personalized approach, 121-22,
    133 n. 14
  responsible, 21-22
  risks himself, 33
  servant role, 20, 112, 122-24
  temptations of, 13, 15-23
  unafraid, 106
Jung, Carl G.
  collective unconscious, 30, 116
  infantile memories, 131 n. 4
  middle age, 40-41
  struggle for meaning, 37
junior executive, 36

Kierkegaard, Sören, 21

Liebman, Joshua, 125 n. 9
life task, 36-46
Lifton, Robert, 128 n. 5
listening, 88
logotherapy
  affirms ultimate meaning, 119
  anti-deterministic, 31
  attitudinal change, 94-95
  challenges philosophy of life,
    115
  compared with Christianity,
    133 n. 9
  distinctiveness in responsibility,
    72

logotherapy—*cont'd*
  deviates from psychoanalysis, 40
  freedom in all circumstances 97-98
  meaning not limited, 86
  noetic reorientation, 110
  supplements psychotherapy, 114
  will to meaning, 47, 121-22
Loomis, Earl, 129 n. 11

MacKinnon, Donald, 128 n. 11 129 n. 1
Markham, Edwin, 27, 32
Martin, Bernard, 129 n. 5
Mary and Martha, 84-91, 113
masculine traits, 40-41
maturity, 13, 16, 69, 79
meaning
  fulfilling, 37
  help in finding, 43-44, 97
  normal concern, 39, 58
  pathways toward, 76
  search for, 47, 62
mental illness, 25, 102, 108
Messiah, 53
miracle drugs, 100
Missildine, Hugh, 130 n. 11
mission, 75
Mitchell, Margaret, 18
moral issue, 56

Nathan, 69
Nietzsche, Frederich, 47
nihilism, 114

noetic, 39-40, 59, 110, 117, 119
noögenic neurosis, 59
nondirective, 43

"Oklahoma," 42
older people, 103
ought, 68-69
Overstreet, Harry
  Cain and Abel, 26
  rich young ruler, 45

paradoxical intention, 130 n. 11, 95-96
paralyzed youth, 55-63, 113, 118
peace of mind, 65
Peter, 74-83, 121, 122
Pharisees, 72, 91, 121
plea for help, 29
pleasure principle, 16-19
power principle, 19-21
Prodigal Son, 52, 91, 116
pseudo-permissiveness, 54
psychic deformation, 17
psychoanalysis
  age of, 30
  compared with logotherapy, 40
  ego psychology, 52
  focused on id, 116
  homeostasis, 65
  inadequacies of, 29, 49, 56, 128 n. 6
  oedipal relationships, 30
  transference, 32
  twofold mistake of, 129 n. 7
  unconscious, 14, 28

psychonoetic antagonism, 31
psychosis, 103-11
psychosomatic medicine, 55

questioned by life, 76
Quisling, 32

relationships, personal, 32, 34, 38,
    52
religious man 14, 119, 127 n. 14
religious therapy, 119
repentance, 79
repressed angel, 23
response, 14
responsibility
    acceptance of, 38, 40, 103
    evasion of, 21-22
    in Christianity, 52, 68, 72, 123
    to find meaning, 76
rich young ruler, 36-46, 113
Rogers, Carl, 88, 127 n. 11
Russia, 37

saintliness, 49
salvation, 35
Samaria, 54
Samaritan woman, 47-54, 56,
    113, 114
Saul, 67
"Say 'Yes' to life," 14, 32
Scheler, Max, 103
self-fulfillment, 64
self-esteem, 19, 109
service, 20, 112

sexual disorders, 67
Simon the Pharisee, 64-73, 113
sin, 55, 59, 66, 73, 100
sinner, 70, 72, 79
spiritual, 30, 40
spiritual vacuum, 47
Standahl, Stanley, 82, 126 n. 9,
    128 n. 12, 129 n. 4
Steinbeck, John, 31
suffering
    contributions of, 92-101
    meaning in, 109
    neurotic, 113
    upward growth, 59
Sullivan, Harry Stack
    at Worcester, 104-5
    euphoria, 65
    miracle of love, 43
    reflected appraisals, 20, 43, 60
    security operations, 28, 116
    self-esteem, 19, 78-99

teachable moment, 32
temptations, 13-21
therapy group, 70, 88
therapeutic situation
    characteristics of, 60-61
    favorable conditions for, 38
Thompson, Dorothy, 17
Thoreau, Henry David, 128 n. 9
Tillich, Paul, 84, 90
togetherness, 91
Tournier, Paul, 81
transcendence, 15, 125 n. 1
Tweedie, Donald, 132 n. 2

unconscious, spiritual, 22, 121

vacuum, existential, 47, 49-50
values
  absolutizing the relative, 119-
    20
  conflicts in, 51, 55-60
  secondary concerns, 50
  spiritual, 18
  supreme, 17, 119
Vienna, 90

Walter, Bruno, 77
Weatherhead, Leslie
  Gerasene demoniac, 105-6
  paralyzed youth, 57
Weisskopf-Joelson, Edith, 49
Whitman, Walt, 93
wholistic psychology, 60
Wise, Carroll, 55, 85, 104,
  126 n. 11
woman, American, 84-86

Zacchaeus, 24-35, 113, 114, 121

SCRIPTURE INDEX

Genesis 4 26

II Samuel 12 69

Psalm 8:5 103

Matthew 4:11b 23
   5:23-24 42
   14:25-33 74
   16:13-19 74-83
   16:25 71
   23:25 72

Mark 2:2-12 55-63
   5:1-20 102-11
   5:25-34 121
   10:13-16 38
   10:17-22 36-46

Luke 4:1-13 13-23
   5:4 75
   5:8 79

7:36-50 64-73
9:51b 88
10:38-42 84-91
15:17 116
19:1-10 24-35
22:24b 113
22:31-34, 54-62 74-83
22:42 19

John 4:4-27 47-54
   5:2-15 92-101
   8:2-11 72
   13:3-5, 12-16 . . . .20, 112-24
   18:10-11 74
   21:4-19 75
   21:15-22 122

Acts 1-5 75

I Corinthians
   12:31b–13:1 89